India's Demographic Dividend and Youth Empowerment

India's Demographic Dividend and Youth Empowerment

Building Blocks for a Youth Policy

Editors

V.S. Vyas

Shreekant Sambrani

ACADEMIC FOUNDATION
NEW DELHI

www.academicfoundation.org

First published in 2017
by

ACADEMIC FOUNDATION
4772-73 / 23 Bharat Ram Road, (23 Ansari Road),
Darya Ganj, New Delhi - 110 002 (India).
Phones : 23245001 / 02 / 03 / 04.
Fax : +91-11-23245005.
E-mail : booksaf@gmail.com
www.academicfoundation.org

Cataloging in Publication Data--DK
Courtesy: D.K. Agencies (P) Ltd. <docinfo@dkagencies.com>

Dialogue with Youth on Education, Health, Livelihood and Citizenship (Consultation) (2016 : Jaipur, India)
India's demographic dividend and youth empowerment : building blocks for a youth policy / editors, V.S . Vyas, Shreekant Sambrani.
pages cm
"The papers in this volume were presented at a Consultation, Dialogue with Youth on Education, Health, Livelihood and Citizenship organised by Ajit Foundation with support from UNICEF and UNFPA ... held in Jaipur on 8 and 9 November 2016"--Acknowledgements.
ISBN 9789332704183

1. Youth--Government policy--India--Congresses. 2. Youth in development--India--Congresses. I. Vyas, V. S., editor. II. Sambrani, Shreekant, editor. III. Ajit Foundation (Jaipur, India), organizer. IV. Title.

HQ799.I5D53 2016 DDC 305.2350954 23

Typeset, printed and bound by The Book Mint, New Delhi.
www.thebookmint.in

Contents

List of Tables and Figures

Tables

Figures

About the Editors/Contributors

Editors:

Vijay Shankar Vyas (*vijaysvyas2108@gmail.com*), is the Chairman of the Ajit Foundation, an institution working for last two decades for empowering youth. He has a PhD in economics and has taught at Bombay University, Sardar Patel University and Indian Institute of Management, Ahmedabad. He was awarded DLitt (*honoris causa*) by Maharana Pratap University of Agricultural Sciences, Udaipur. He was Director of Indian Institute of Management Ahmedabad and Chairman, Governing Board of the Institute of Development Studies, Jaipur. He has been Senior Advisor in the World Bank, Member of the Economic Advisory Council of the Prime Minister, Member of the Central Board of Reserve Bank of India and Deputy Chairman of the State Planning Board of Rajasthan. He was awarded Padma Bhushan in 2006 by the President of India.

Shreekant Sambrani (*shreekant.sambrani@gmail.com*) is an engineer (Indian Institute of Technology, Bombay/Northwestern University) and an economist (Cornell University). He is a management researcher/adviser. He was earlier Professor at Indian Institute of Management, Ahmedabad, Chief of the Research Bureau, The Economic Times and Founder-Director, Institute of Rural Management, Anand. He has advised numerous private, co-operative, government and international agencies on policy and strategy issues. He also writes on current events of social, political and economic significance.

Contributors:

Aditi Gupta (*aditigupta86@gmail.com*) is associated with Vidya Bhavan, an educational institution inspired by Gandhian values. An engineer from Indian Institute of Technology Delhi, and MBA from Stanford University, she has been involved in the development sector for six years now, working in various non-profit organisations. Currently, she is working as a strategy consultant with the Vidya Bhawan Society.

Pawan Gupta (*pawansidh@gmail.com*) is the founder of the Society for Integrated Development of Himalayas (SIDH). Inspired by Gandhian philosophy in education and in rural development, SIDH is conducting experiments in the rural areas of Himachal Pradesh to make education more meaningful and relevant.

Amit Kumar (*kigs_in@yahoo.com*) is Project Director, Kumarappa Institute of Gram Swaraj, Jaipur. He has been working in the field of rural development and socio-economic research for more than 15 years. He has supervised more than 30 international internships and has several published papers to his credit.

Kanchan Mathur (*mathurkanchan@idaho.org*) is Professor at the Institute of Development Studies, Jaipur. She has wide experience of research, training, consultancy and advocacy in issues related to gender and development in India and South Asia. She has published books and papers in India and abroad on gender related issues.

Ajay Mehta (*ajaysinghmehta1954@gmail.co*) is associated with Vidya Bhavan, an educational institution inspired by Gandhian values. Trained in economics (BA Yale University and MPhil, Jawaharlal Nehru University), he is on the governing body of Vidya Bhawan and Seva Mandir, organisations dedicated to support civil society initiatives.

Anju Dhadda Mishra (*anjudhaddamisra@gmail.com*) is a poet, educationist and author. She has taught English to college students and has guided research for over three decades. She has published extensively on literary issues; and is a recipient of Rajasthan Sahitya Academy's Sudhindra award for poetry.

Sweta Mishra (*sweta.mishra1@gmail.com*) is the Team Leader of the Technical Support Unit, Sports and Youth Services Department, Government of Odisha. She has been closely associated with the formulation and monitoring of the Odisha Youth Policy.

S. Mohanakumar (*mohanakumar.s@gmail.com*), has a PhD in Economics. He is an Associate Professor in the Institute of Development Studies, Jaipur. He works in the areas of political economy, decentralisation and livelihood issues, especially in relation to Kerala.

Prabhat Pankaj (*prabhat.pankaj@jaipuria.ac.in*) is Director, Jaipuria Institute of Management, Jaipur. He has a PhD in applied economics. He has been teaching economics in universities and business schools in India and abroad. His recent research engagement is in the area of happiness, and on innovation in teaching of economics.

PRAVAH (*pravah@ndf.vsnl.net.in*) and **ComMutiny Youth Collective** (CYC) (*cyc.delhi@gmai.com*) have spearheaded youth-led social action campaigns, addressing issues of discrimination, governance, gender-based violence, inclusion etc. Through these campaigns CYC and PRAVAH have been able to reach a large number of young people through workshops and events.

Sanjay Sharma (*sanjay17sharma@gmail.com*) is a senior journalist based in Chandigarh. He is a keen observer of the economic and political scene in Punjab. He has worked as correspondent for BBC.

Acknowledgements

The papers in this volume were presented at a Consultation, "Dialogue with Youth on Education, Health, Livelihood and Citizenship" organised by Ajit Foundation with support from UNICEF and UNFPA. The Consultation was held in Jaipur on 8 and 9 November 2016. We are grateful to Samuel Mawunganidze and Sulagna Roy from UNICEF, and Sunil Jacob from UNFPA, Rajasthan for their excellent support.

A distinguished Advisory Committee comprising Nikhil Dey, G. Girdhar, Shiv Kumar, Vijay Mahajan, Ajay Mehta, Prabhat Pankaj, Aparna Sahay, and Vikram Vyas guided the Consultation. An energetic team of Laxmi Vyas, Ashok Bapana, Anju Dhadda Misra, Mohammad Iqbal, Amit Kumar, Jaipal Kaushik, Mansee Choudhary and Geeta Garwa undertook organisational responsibilities. Rajesh Sharma, Sanjay Gupta and Sanjay Shrimali provided excellent administrative support.

The book is a collection of papers by authors who have given deep thought to the issues facing the youth of this country. The rapporteur Anju Dhadda Misra has ably captured the substance of the authors' contributions and deliberations of the Consultation. Sanu Kapila and Sona Kapila from Academic Foundation took up the production of the book on priority basis despite their other commitments.

The participation of a number of alert youth from schools, colleges and universities and the group of their distinguished mentors, Rajendra Bhanawat, Narendra Gupta, Prabhat Pankaj, Jaipal Singh, Pawan Gupta, K.L. Sharma and Ashraf Patel made the whole effort more meaningful.

I hope the efforts and involvement of all these friends and colleagues will contribute to the empowerment of India's youth.

—V.S. Vyas
Chairman
Ajit Foundation

V.S. VYAS

Introduction

India has the advantage of a very large young population. Nearly 60 per cent of the country's population is in the age group 16 to 34. With such a demographic structure, two advantages are quite obvious. One, a very large productive workforce is available in the country, and two, the proportion of non-working people, those in the age groups of 0 to 15 and of 60 and above, is much less. This is said to be the demographic dividend that India can avail of. It should be recognised that the advantage that country has is largely in terms of the potential. The reality is not that encouraging. In order to take advantage of the demographic dividend and help channelise the energy of the youth to build a better future for themselves and for the country, attention must be focussed on this large young population.

Youth in India do not have the advantage of an enlightening and meaningful education. The proportion of students who complete secondary education, which can be considered as the minimum qualification for higher education or for entry to any modern occupation, is very low. On the content and quality of the education, there is great deal of dissatisfaction in every section of society. It is generally agreed that the present education system, apart from several other defects, does not encourage a work culture; if anything, it discourages manual work. In this context, the recent emphasis on skill development is welcome, but skill development by itself without a sound base of elementary and secondary education is not adequate.

Employment prospects are not very bright even for the youth who have received some education and training for certain occupations. The rate of job creation is highly inadequate compared to the number of youth entering in the labour market. The situation is worse for those who are illiterate or semi-literate and unskilled. A large number of youth are frustrated and driven to drug addiction and other anti-social activities because of unemployment and bleak future prospects.

The education system and the current social and cultural environment do not encourage what may be considered as essential qualities of good citizenship. A healthy society requires its youth to be socially responsible, sensitive to the plight of the disadvantaged, and appreciative of the diversity of its culture. Therefore, a sound youth policy should address not only the problems of education, health and livelihood, but also aim at making youth good citizens. The urgency of moving in these directions becomes apparent once we realise that the bulge in the youth population is not a permanent feature of our demography. The bulge in the age group 15-24 will start shrinking after 2025. In another 20 years or so, we will also face a rise in the proportion of people in the higher age groups. There is only a limited time to reap what is popularly called the demographic dividend. The Central government and a few State governments have formulated youth policies prompted by these considerations. Some other states are also contemplating to design policies for their youth.

The Ajit Foundation recently organised a consultation titled "Dialogue with Youth", with support from United Nations International Emergency Fund (UNICEF) and United Nations Population Fund (UNFPA). A group of concerned citizens and a number of enlightened youth met to discuss what could be the important ingredients of a youth policy for our country.

The group looked into objectives enunciated in the Centre's youth policy, namely to:

i. create a productive workforce that can make a sustainable contribution to India's economic development;
ii. develop a strong and healthy generation equipped to take up future challenges;
iii. instil social values and promote community service to build national ownership;
iv. facilitate participation and civic engagement at all levels of governance; and
v. support youth at risk and create equitable opportunities for all disadvantaged and marginalised youth.

While endorsing these objectives, it was felt that there should be recognition of the diversity of youth population and clarity on key issues that concern the youth. A unique feature of this consultation was the emphasis on hearing youth, who are the main stakeholders, and to understand their perspectives on education, health, livelihood and citizenship. This was all the more necessary because there is a wide gap in the age group of policymakers and the present generation of youth.

Some of the academics and activists spelled out concerns in these areas and offered solutions from different perspectives, ranging from the Gandhian, to the liberal-managerial and finally of the grass roots workers, in the papers they submitted for discussion. The group also had the advantage of a few case studies focussing on specific problems faced by youth in select states. These problems, such as drug addiction among the youth in Punjab, severe unemployment among the highly educated youth in Kerala, social backwardness and gender discrimination in Rajasthan, were discussed in the case studies. Another study looked into the process of formulation of the youth policy and arrangements for its monitoring in a state, namely Odisha.

The papers and case studies discussed in the Consultation are included in this volume. Based on the views expressed in the background paper and case studies, and the discussion with youth in smaller working groups, some important suggestions were culled out, which are presented in the last chapter of the book. These could serve as meaningful inputs for framing a youth policy in the country and the states, especially in the areas of education, health, livelihood and citizenship. The papers and the case studies are briefly introduced in the following paragraphs.

Pawan Gupta, an eminent Gandhian thinker and founder of Society for Integrated Development of Himalayas, argues with emphasis in his paper "The Unbearable Burden of Modernity" that before attempting any policy for youth, we need to understand their psychology, beliefs and aspirations. The youth in the country are suffering from self-negation and frustration, mainly due to a lack of self-confidence. Under enormous pressure to appear developed and smart, the youth are losing their identity. They need to be freed from the heavy burden of appearances. They should have confidence, though not vanity or a false sense of superiority.

Education should help the youth to discover themselves, to be natural. It should inculcate a sense of self-esteem. While imparting education to youth, Gupta maintains, we should be cognizant of the fact that understanding and learning are different from each other, and that information cannot be equated with knowledge. But today information is being disseminated in the name of knowledge.

The author notes that there is no reason for the youth of this country to feel inferior to their western counterparts. It should be remembered that historically India, though an agrarian society, was fairly advanced in industry also. Until the 1750s, India was producing nearly one-fourth of the world's total output of non-agricultural products. And that was not produced in large enterprises, but in small village and cottage units. To give meaningful employment to the youth today, we need to make space for the different types of smaller industrial units and develop comparative advantages for them, by training youth to start and manage such enterprises. Industrial policies should be geared to support these units and remove hurdles in their growth. Larger industries should share responsibilities of training youth and providing opportunities for their growth to the extent necessary.

The paper by Aditi Gupta and Ajay Mehta, titled "Youth Policy: Dialogue with Youth", provides an insightful discussion of the real locus of a policy, dangers of over-dependence on government, and the importance of caring for and listening to youth in educational institutions. The authors argue that right policies can contribute to change that is pervasive and significant. However, policy alone cannot fix our social problems. Real change happens at the level of the individual and the community, in day-to-day decisions made by them. It happens when the locus of change is among the ordinary people, and they consider themselves responsible for the content and outcome of a policy. The authors suggest that before announcing a policy, we should take into account possible responses of individuals, communities and organisations likely to be affected. By focusing on policies to be framed at the top, we may be teaching our youth that the solutions to their problems lie outside them, with people who hold power.

The authors also maintain that an organisation's dependence on government might result in an undesirable shift in priorities and cause unhealthy power dynamics within it. They illustrate these tendencies by citing the case of Vidya Bhawan, an 85-year old civil society institution in Udaipur who started with the objective of imparting inclusive, all-round and value based education. It is a consortium of 13 institutions, including schools, teacher training colleges, graduate and post-graduate colleges and research institutions. The paper gives a short and pithy account of how this institution based on Gandhian values and ideals got corrupted once it started receiving large government grants. These grants ushered in bureaucratic culture in their wake, made workers self-seekers, and eroded the community spirit. The institution started sliding down a slippery path. An intervention of its old students, who had received value-based education, was needed to correct the path taken by their alma mater.

Citing the case of suicide by a frustrated girl student, the authors stress the need to bring teachers and students closer to enable them to build relationships based on mutual trust and respect, and to develop a culture of regular discussion and consensus-building. Only then can an individual's problems in his/her specific context can be taken into account, and such tragic incidences avoided.

Prabhat Pankaj, director of a renowned management institution, presents an outline of the youth policy in his paper "Youth Policy for Young India: Towards a Millennium-Friendly Youth Policy". He says that youth policy must take cognizance of the fact that our young generation is greatly influenced by global forces. His paper is based on two premises: i) inclusiveness of youth in the process of developing the policy; and ii) evaluation of programmes and policies on the criterion of their benefits to youth. These should be the hallmarks of any youth policy.

Surveying the present situation, he maintains that our education system is not keeping pace with the times; a large employability gap exists; there is a big learning deficit; the system is not capable of dealing with problems of first-generation learners; there is a rural-urban gap in the access to as well as quality of education; such gaps also prevail in education facilities for different social groups. In this context, he pleads for faster adoption and assimilation of technology on the one hand and increasing what he terms as happiness quotient for the youth i.e., promoting happiness-enhancing activities and practices among them.

The author says that policy formation should be preceded by a survey of the youth to map their aspirations. The policy should emphasise over-hauling education delivery systems which will involve a major shift from teacher-centric to student-centric education; greater use of technology-enabled learning; skill-building and employability enhancement as mandatory parts of delivery at schools and colleges; special emphasis on building non-cognitive skills such as grit, teamwork, optimism and a growth-oriented mindset. He lays special emphasis on health and happiness and suggests that a survey should be conducted to measure happiness among youth.

The author's diagnosis of the problems facing youth and his suggestions gain credibility as they are based on a survey of the youth, mainly the students.

The theme of the paper presented by ComMutiny, The Youth Collective (CYC) and PRAVAH, a consortium of 30 like-minded professionals from several organisations working with young people, was how to make sustainable long-term progress on sticky social issues. The paper begins with the assertion that change by itself need not necessarily lead to improvement. One can cite examples of various changes taking place in the nation's capital. For example, the metro system was meant to bring down traffic congestion and high pollution levels. Strong laws against gender violence were supposed to make the city safer. Attracting a lot of industry and corporates to National Capital Region (NCR, Delhi and its satellite towns) was touted as a sure way of creating jobs and reducing inequality. Yet Delhi remains among the top five polluted cities in the world, with one of the worst traffic congestion. It continues to have an abysmal record on gender violence and is sometimes called the rape capital of the world. Unemployment in NCR is higher than the national average. Delhi has the second highest level of inequality in the world after Johannesburg in South Africa.

The country is grappling with myriad social problems ranging from sanitation to intolerance to inequality. Despite several efforts coupled with resource provision, the paper maintains, we have yet to make a sustainable dent in resolving these issues. Obviously we are missing a piece of the puzzle. The paper mentions a different approach to social issues which CYC and PRAVAH have been experimenting with. It is the psycho-social or an inside-out approach, i.e., a way to usher in change by changing the mindset.

The paper reports results of a survey to validate the inside-out approach to change. CYC and its associates decided to test whether the narrative on social change theories was itself undergoing a change. For this purpose, they conducted a social change narrative survey to map the kind of interventions or solutions people believed were required to solve major social problems the country faces. The survey consisted of five questions on five major social issues: low literacy, religious intolerance, gender discrimination, unemployment, and sanitation. Each issue had four solutions, namely: psycho-social, legal, infrastructure and systemic/policy based ones. Respondents had to pick the best possible solution or the combination of solutions to solve these issues.

The survey results showed that across all the five issues and each of the diverse demographic groups, the psycho-social approach was rated the highest. In other words, respondents felt that mindset change is the most important intervention to resolve any of these issues. The respondents made it clear that without mindset change, simply making laws and policies and creating infrastructure would not help.

PRAVAH, an institution working with youth for more than two decades, presented a paper titled, "Abilities Beyond Skills: A Curriculum on Life Competencies for Employability". India has to deal with the challenge of gainfully employing millions of young people entering the workforce every year to reap its demographic dividend. For this reason, it is imperative that those entering the job market are adequately prepared. This implies, as the paper puts, "they (should) have the knowledge, skills, attitudes and behaviours, a person needs to get work, stay in work, do their job well and reach their fullest potential." The paper quotes an impact assessment of the efforts for training initiative led by National Skill Development Corporation and partner organisations. It revealed that a mismatch between training and job requirements is pushing up the drop-out rate. On the one hand, there is huge unemployment, and on the other, employers are unable to find the right type of persons for the jobs they could offer.

PRAVAH's efforts in this direction are aimed at supplementing training in technical skills. They point out that employability should refer to knowledge, skills, attitudes and behaviour. An employer will look for people who, in addition to technical skills, have attributes such as capacity and willingness to take responsibility, capacity to imbibe new knowledge, abilities of conflict-resolution and problem-solving, effective communication, decision-making, leadership and teamwork. These are the competencies that enable a person to perform well and contribute effectively to the organisation.

From young people's perspective, the training should enable them to lead meaningful and productive lives. They are not just seeking a livelihood but are also aspiring for a fulfilling career, a career where a person is able to discover his/her full potential, grow professionally and develop as a human being, to contribute more effectively, and to perform well. The paper argues for the need to expand the scope of skills development programmes in order to enhance employability in the wider sense of the term. The success of these programmes should be judged not merely in terms of numbers placed, but also in terms of how individuals have grown in their chosen jobs/careers over time and how satisfied they are, with the overall quality of their life. These criteria are relevant for employees as well as the self-employed.

The paper informs that PRAVAH is in the process of developing an alternative youth-centric curriculum in partnership with UNFPA and CYC, called ABS (abilities beyond skills). Its objective is to bridge the gap between expectations of potential employers and employees, and equip potential employees with flexible, wholesome leadership values, attitudes, behaviours and decision-making capacities. It is expected to be rolled out parallel to the domain curriculum, or can be integrated into the ongoing vocational training. Its stress is on: i) values, attitude and behaviour; ii) effective decision-making; and iii) alignment with social realities. All the three modules are integrated to help the trainee develop an all-round personality together with needed skills and competencies. It is proposed to work with trainers of skilling agencies, provide them these modules, and training and hand-holding support so that they can effectively run the ABS curriculum along with their technical courses.

For a wider understanding of some of the issues facing youth in different parts of the country, case studies of four states are included in the volume. The first of these, "Drug Addiction in Punjab: Genesis and Prescription" by Sanjay Sharma, attempts to define the root cause of the vulnerability of the youth of Punjab to substance abuse and measures to fight this menace. After documenting extensive use of drugs as reported by different sources, he laments that though the problem is very serious, the approach to handle it is casual, and based on hearsay and unscientific data. The first requirement, according to him, therefore is that the State government should commission a scientific survey and an in-depth study, focussing on the extent of the malady and its roots.

The paper emphasises the role of education in fighting the drug abuse. Quality education at affordable cost should be within the reach of each individual. Education should aim at making youth employable, and, at the same time, make them conscious of their true cultural heritage. In popular media, Punjabi culture is depicted as Bohemian, and drinking as its hallmark. This is a twisted version of Punjab. In fact, Punjabi culture sets high value on equality and justice. Distortions have set in because of growing disparities in wealth and incomes. Political, economic and social power is getting concentrated in a few hands, and vested interests control the means of communication, particularly the media. They encourage intolerance. Any questioning of prevailing religious and social norms invites harassment and criminal cases on the grounds of hurting religious sentiments.

The youth should be encouraged to raise questions and find solutions. They should learn that Punjabis make good entrepreneurs. They are less dogmatic and believe in hard work rather than in miracles. To usher in such cultural changes, the government must engage with progressive civil and religious organisations. Change in the outlook of the youth will help fight drug abuse.

In order to save the youth from drug abuse, the author suggests that the State government needs to create a string of medical centres, which may be attached to schools, colleges and youth organisations. Medical reports from the state suggest that at least one of six addicts wants to be cured. There is evidence that psychological tests can predict vulnerability to drugs at an early stage. The proposed centres, which should become part of regular medical services, should have facilities to identify individuals who are likely to fall prey to drug abuse, and medical support should be made available to them.

The paper reports that youth sent to drug de-addiction centres are not always welcomed back in the society and remain socially isolated and unemployed. The government should devise a strategy for their full rehabilitation in the society and gainful employment.

A new initiative involving civil society at the grass roots to fight drug menace is required. Village or *mohalla* level anti-drug committees need to be formed. They should be empowered to report drug availability, and monitor health and education facilities from the perspective of fighting drug abuse at the local level. They should be enabled to rehabilitate people who want to come out of addiction. These committees will be capable of creating social awareness and isolating those involved in drug trade, who will be afraid to face representatives of their local community. The same committees can also keep an eye on the cultural and social practices that promote drugs and devise strategies to discourage these.

While the major focus should be on curtailing the demand, vigorous efforts should also be made to control the sources of supplies. Drug inspection machinery in the health department needs to be substantially strengthened to fight organised drug suppliers. Drug inspectors should also be adequately trained to keep an eye on pharmaceutical companies, which may sell drugs under false labels. The author suggests that relations with Afghanistan, Pakistan, countries of Central Asia and Iran should be improved to control drug cartels, operating from these countries.

S. Mohanakumar, an academic from Kerala now with the Institute of Development Studies, Jaipur, presents a case study entitled "Demographic Transition and Employability in Kerala". He said that the current phase of demographic transition in Kerala is characterised by the growth of older population while population in the age group 0-14 has been declining. The rate of growth of population in the working age group is rising, but rather slowly. The Kerala decadal population growth is 4.9 per cent as compared to the national figure of 17.1 per cent. The state has moved towards zero population growth during 2001-2011. The demographic transition in the state is accompanied by a relatively high proportion of female job-seekers, which may be due to the appreciably higher sex ratio, 1,084 females per 1,000 males as against the national average of 943.

He maintains that the debate on demographic dividend is primarily carried out in binary terms, whether the higher proportion of young population is a blessing or a threat to the country. What is more important is to find how the country taps the productiveness of its young population by designing policies, programmes and schemes to actively engage them in the labour market in a manner that is also satisfying to them. As youth is nurtured in different social and economic groups, cultures and milieus, their aspirations are too diversified to scale down into a single and uniform mode of intervention.

Analysing the prospects of youth in Kerala, the author suggests that the number of live registrations of job-seekers with employment exchanges can be taken as a crude index of unemployment. In 2015, there were 3.6 million job-seekers, more than half of whom were females. Only 5 per cent of the job-seekers had technical or professional qualifications, while 95 per cent had only general education with little specific skill. IT certificate-holders and engineering diploma-holders constituted more than 80 per cent of the technically qualified job-seekers. Their numbers have been on the rise. There were also job-seekers with engineering and medical degrees.

These trends and patterns in Kerala reveal shortages of employable skills even among job-seekers with technical and professional degrees. This scenario of poorly-conducted vocational courses along with deficient higher education is known as the two-box-disease and indicates a divorce between vocational training and higher education resulting in highly educated youth remaining non-employable.

The author evaluates the effectiveness of different programmes of the State and Central governments in skilling the job-seekers and youth. He raises three questions: i) what type of skills does the productive sector of the economy require to absorb the unemployed youth? ii) what skills do the job-seekers possess? and iii) what should be the rate of growth of each sector to absorb the reserve labour force?

Looking to the prospects of labour absorption in different sectors, he points out that the current scenario of the farm sector dissuades youth from looking into it as a source of employment for two reasons: i) there is already an overcrowding in agriculture; the SGDP (state gross domestic product) from agriculture and allied activities is only 11 per cent, but over 20 per cent of the workforce is engaged in it; ii) there is a mismatch between the skill content of the labour remaining unemployed and the type of work available in crop production or allied sectors. The secondary sector is a potential avenue of absorbing a large mass of the unemployed youth in the state; however, the share of manufacturing in the SGDP is very small. The bulk of the SGDP is contributed by services. This is a broad term encompassing several types of activities requiring varied skills, which have been undergoing transformation.

Two questions thus emerge: i) can the two-box-disease be addressed by upgrading and sophisticating the infrastructure of the vocational training institutions of Kerala? ii) does the prevailing higher education, especially technical education, need change or overhauling and if so, in which direction and in what mode? It is also important to examine as to why there is a large inflow of manual and semi-skilled youth from other states into Kerala, what type of jobs do the migrant labour from Kerala perform in West Asia and how are their skills different from those migrating to Kerala. The author concludes that if multiple issues faced by the youth of Kerala are not resolved, the demographic dividend might prove a curse rather than a blessing.

Kanchan Mathur, Professor at Institute of Development Studies, Jaipur presented, "Exploring Education, Employment and Citizenship: A Case Study of Youth in Rajasthan". Her paper critically analyses issues related to youth in the state. It argues that given the distinct socio-cultural reality of the state, it is pertinent to view youth not as a homogenous group but through the subgroups of caste, class and gender. She documents the male-female disparities in education, health and social relationships. Similar disparities also exist between the urban and the rural youth.

Can the quality of education and skill upgradation schemes being offered to young women and men lead to employment opportunities that provide secure livelihoods, is the key issue the paper addresses while exploring the position of the youth in education, employment and citizenship in the state. It is evident that there are vast expectations from this large segment of the population. How can the youth become alert citizens, capable of being change agents? How can they be prepared to take up socially responsible roles? How can their energy be enhanced?

The paper examines the social, economic and cultural context of the state. It attempts a situational analysis of the youth in the state to highlight the disparities in young women and men's access to education, opportunities for employment and livelihoods and examines the skill development schemes made available by the State government. The concluding part of the paper puts together case studies of organisations working with youth in the state and suggests measures to better address the issues of youth.

The author underscores the point that a deeper understanding of the biological, social and cultural dimensions of young women's and men's lives could facilitate the design of programmes that would not only support them but help them become parts of solutions to contemporary challenges.

In another case study of the youth in Rajasthan, "Perceptions of Rural Rajasthani Youth: Education, Livelihood, Citizenship", carried out in a *panchayat* of Jaipur district, the author Amit Kumar from Kumarappa Institute for Rural Development focuses on rural youth of the state. He identifies two major forces of change impacting the rural youth: rapid development of transport and communication facilities and consequent inroads of urban culture in villages on the one hand, and spread of modern education to rural areas on the other. He examines the impact of these changes on livelihood patterns. He also dwells on the nature of involvement of youth in local politics.

The author notes that as in other parts of the country, the spread of roads, apart from importing urban lifestyles, has resulted in a decline of household and cottage enterprises, as they are unable to withstand competition from large-scale urban industries. But it has also given rise to new occupations catering to the lifestyles of rural households changing under the influence of urban culture. He also draws attention to another major development, a rise in the land value in the vicinity of roads. This has led to sale of such land for housing or industrial purposes. The author reports that the money the farmer households receive from such sales is rarely invested but squandered in unproductive expenditure on flashy lifestyles.

The spread of education in rural areas is limited to primary or at best post-primary schooling. There are few institutions of secondary education. Girls' enrolment even in primary schools is disproportionately low; in secondary schools, it goes down further. The quality of education is very unsatisfactory. The students are not enthusiastic about the education they receive. It does not equip them with useful skills, which could help them in earning a decent income. But their aspiration levels are enhanced. This has resulted in a new kind of employment among the educated youth, what the author calls commissioning, i.e., to work as intermediaries and earn commission rather than soil one's hand with hard labour.

The author finds that the rural youth in the area surveyed are politically aware, though they would vote only for the candidate from their own community. However, they would not be keen to participate in elections as candidates, since scions of more affluent sections monopolise the space. It would be possible for them to enter politics through *panchayats*, but they are highly politicised and dominated by one or the other of the two principal parties of the state. As a result, leaders of the dominant party in the village misuse the forum of the *gram sabha*. Its proceedings are not shared with the villagers. Overall, the youth have a narrow and cynical view of the local politics.

Based on his observations, the author recommends that value-based education should be given priority, with emphasis on the dignity of labour. The youth should be trained in skills that ensure decent jobs; small, decentralised industries should be emphasised. This should be reflected in institutional support to such units. The youth should be encouraged to participate in local government and learn the basics of politics at the grass roots.

Sweta Mishra, currently working as team leader, Technical Support Unit, State Youth Welfare Board, Government of Odisha, a key participant in the youth policy formulation in Odisha, presents the case study, "Odisha Youth Policy: Tracing the Journey, from Formulation to Implementation". Odisha is one among the few states that have formulated an explicit youth policy, several features of which are unique and need to be underlined. The State government launched the policy in April 2013. Its overarching goal is to engage, enable and empower youth to be partners in the development process.

The policy was developed through a participatory process, with the objective of making it youth-centric and capturing the needs and aspirations of the youth with a bottom-up approach. UNFPA, Odisha, partnered the State government and guided policy development to ensure a participatory exercise. The process was designed with a systematic approach entailing an extensive qualitative study and a series of consultation meetings with key constituents, stakeholders and special groups.

The author reports that the policy has been translated into a comprehensive plan of action with specific programmes and activities under each thematic area along with well-defined roles and responsibilities of the respective departments. It contains 74 directives across 9 priority sectors. Twenty-one line departments, some of which already have significant components of programmes/ schemes for youth development, are responsible for implementation of policy directives in their respective domains. There are built-in provisions for inter-sectoral co-ordination, convergence of programmes and resources, and synergy in action. The State department of sports and youth services is designated as the nodal agency for tracking implementation of policy directives.

A unique feature of the policy is that a high power committee, under the chairmanship of the chief minister, has been formed to review the implementation on a half-yearly basis. A task force has been formed under the chairmanship of the chief secretary to review the progress on a quarterly basis. A technical support unit for tracking the implementation has been established in the department of sports and youth services with support from UNFPA. With its participatory formulation and detailed arrangements for implementation, the Odisha model of youth policy is something other states could follow.

The authors of the papers from varied backgrounds looked into issues facing the youth from different perspectives. Some aspects, however, have been emphasised by many or all of them:

- *First*, they all recognise that India has an initial edge with a large proportion of youth in its population. But this is just a potential advantage and can be actualised only by empowering and enlightening the youth. In any event, it is not a permanent advantage, since in 10 years or so, the bulge in youth population will disappear.
- *Second*, the young population will prove to be an asset if they are properly educated, have healthy, anxiety-free lives with assured productive employment and are capable of discharging the role of good citizens.
- *Third*, education is the foundation on which an alert, capable, and productive young generation can be raised.
- *Fourth*, education should provide what a contributor calls "abilities beyond skills."
- *Fifth*, the state and the society should provide space to the youth to socialise, learn and innovate in their own ways. Too

many constrains, howsoever well meaning, will harm the development of the youth.

- *Sixth*, the state has a major, though not the sole, responsibility of providing right opportunities for growth to the youth. This is the rationale for a youth policy at the Central and State levels.
- *Seventh*, policy formation should follow a participatory mode to take into account the views and aspirations of the youth.
- *Eighth*, the policy should recognise social and economic diversities in the background of the youth.
- *Ninth*, the importance of the youth policy for the state should be reflected in a visible involvement of the top functionaries of the state.
- *Tenth*, the policy should clearly define the roles and responsibilities of the youth themselves, their family and their community.

1

PAWAN K. GUPTA

The Unbearable Burden of Modernity

Distorted Concept of Education

As a country, we suffer from an acute sense of diffidence (*atma-sankoch*). This is in turn related to a tendency to mindlessly imitate without examining what we have assumed to be superior, a loss of self confidence and a perpetual anxiety to look/appear good and seek others' approval. This is manifest in sophisticated, subtle and refined as well as the most vulgar and crude forms of imitation. It is perpetuated largely by the education system we have borrowed from elsewhere and are now busy universalising it. Such education has no roots; it ignores or abhors both the civilisational and cultural moorings. We have even enacted the right to education without defining what education is! It is assumed to be what is served in schools recognised by the State or the Constitution. After all, the Constitution is our new God.

Youth are the worst sufferers of this malaise. Mahatma Gandhi repeatedly drew the country's attention to this huge problem, but few seem to have understood him in totality. Very few, least of all the State, understand the distinction he made between the law (*vidhi*) and the eternal principles (*sanaatan vidhaan*). For him the eternal principles were paramount. But not for us; for us it is the manmade Constitution. Therefore, education is as defined, or rather imposed, by the State.

There is hardly any point in lamenting the past, but it can help us diagnose the problem and perhaps provide pointers to regaining self-confidence. The huge problem affecting first and foremost our substantial younger population needs to be addressed. And we need a policy that will aim at not just the immediate problem, but more importantly, its long term resolution as well. That will involve stemming those forces and tendencies from where such issues arise, leading to regeneration of self-respect, self-image, self-confidence and creativity.

A sense of self-respect and pride in one's work is an important area to which the State policy must give adequate attention. Normally our policies only look at the tangible, or quantifiable aspects. But the other dimensions, the intangible—pride, dignity and self-respect—are more important. Once they are actualised, they take an energy of their own. That is self-motivation.

We have some experience of this, based on which one can say with full confidence that this is doable. The State will have to take care of the material aspect, the hardware, but the other aspects, the intangible (self-respect, dignity, taking pride in one's work, confidence, a sense of ownership and social responsibility, among others) has to be thought of and planned carefully by involving the people.

What are usually given in the guise of providing soft skills and personality development are a rudimentary knowledge of English and training in some manners. Normally good manners are as defined by the West, so we teach how to shake hands and say hello, or wear the (western) dress properly. This approach does not generate true self-confidence among the youth; instead, it infuses them with a deep (but hidden) sense of shame (of their ownselves, their culture, their home and parents, their mother tongue), resulting in an acute sense of inferiority. Listen to the public announcements at major airports and on airlines in the country—in foreign-accented English, when we have a perfectly understandable Indian accent better suited to the milieu of the country. Even Hindi announcements are as if spoken by a foreigner.

The Intangibles

We need to distinguish between the relative (based on comparison—*sapeksha*) and the true or absolute (*nirapeksha*) self-confidence. The entire education system is geared to enhance the relative self-confidence, if it does anything at all. This is counter-productive. Self confidence in our country is by and large equated with speaking 'good' English, certain 'style' (as decided by the market and fashion industry) and 'smartness' (not defined, but perhaps cleverness of a kind). This is at the cost of our ways and our languages. The process is self-defeating because the person starts hiding his cultural identity and mindlessly imitates what is taught under the garb of personality development. To gain true confidence, one needs to feel good about oneself, one's cultural background (this does not mean not appreciating other cultures and other languages). This can be done by challenging certain false beliefs hidden below the surface, assumptions and myths about what is 'good', 'superior/inferior' and other such value-judgements.

Every situation is defined by two parameters: its statics (*sthiti*) and its dynamics (*gati*). All feelings, knowledge, beliefs or assumptions are static and unmanifested. Their expression, the manifested aspect is dynamic. So a feeling of respect/disrespect is statics and its expression through an action (conscious or unconscious), such as touching someone else's feet, saying *namaskar* or hello is its dynamics. The meaning within is statics while the word without is dynamics. The entire present focus (the appearance, the manifested aspect) is on the dynamics and statics is completely ignored. We need major programmes, built into our school and college curricula if possible, to help young people understand and appreciate the distinction between the two aspects.

Words are distinct from meanings. They are only indicative of the meaning, which is the reality, whether we understand it or not. Our priority objective must be the meaning which is beyond language. Words are a construct to depict it. They are restricted by the language. Meaning has a higher value than words but modern education perpetuates the myth that words are meanings and they are the same and synonymous. If this distinction is not clear, we get trapped by words. And the meaning that gets imposed (or sometimes is imposed) on these words—as different from the real (existential) meaning—unconsciously starts dominating our thinking.

Modernity is adept at creating such confusions between reality and constructs between the objective and the means, between the real and the apparent. So modern categories have assumed or imposed meanings as different from the reality. Instead of using categories for our purpose, we start getting used by the categories. This gives modernity power over our minds, over our aspirations, desires and thus over our actions.

The paradigm of values or the paradigm of definitive meaning is different from the paradigm of price or the provisional meaning. Values are based on reality. They are absolute while the other is an imposition based on comparison, relative. Values are fixed, definitive and intrinsic and beyond time and space. They do not depend on the individual or societal preferences. The paradigm of price, taste and opinion depends on external factors and is impacted among others by both time and space. To illustrate, the value of clothing is its ability to protect the body, but our preference for a particular kind of clothing is a matter of personal choice.

Modern education creates confusion between these two paradigms by equating them, thus overstating price or the transient or the provisional and understating value or the definitive paradigm. This confusion has many manifestations.

Words get equated with or even supersede meanings. Understanding the other gets confused with agreeing with the other. Training is equated and confused with education, information with knowledge. Empirical/traditional knowledge is labeled as superstition. Subjects and categories take precedence over the objective or knowledge and experience. No distinction is made between believing and assuming (without knowing) and knowing. Perceiving is equated with knowing, the provisional with the definitive, appearance (*lagana*) or doing (*karna*) with being (*hona*), arrogance with self-esteem; relative confidence (*sapeksha atma vishwas*) with absolute self-belief (*nirapeksha atma vishwas*); licence (*man marzi*) with freedom (self-organised *swatantrata*); reasoning and logic with experiencing and understanding; ideology (a category) with philosophy (*darshan*, which is beyond category); different with opposite; and 'development' with real progress/achievement.

This is how modern myth is created—at one level it falsely equates higher value with a lower one by imposing the transient. It also creates artificial dichotomies. This starts in school when we teach the 'opposites': black versus white; day versus night. But it does not stop there. It goes on: man versus woman, boy versus girl, east versus west and later on, goes on to Hindu versus Muslim, developed versus undeveloped and so on. Adjectives are also a big problem if we do not teach them with the warning that they are relative, that they are subjective and are not value-judgments in themselves.

Modern science has cast its influence on all disciplines of learning. It overemphasises reasoning. It has conditioned the mind to be satisfied merely with an apparently reasonable sounding answer to the why. This is another obstacle to seeing reality in its entirety. Observing and experiencing a phenomenon in its totality is not appreciated while a partial answer to why satisfies people 'trained' in modern education. We are conditioned to think we know when actually we only believe or assume. The overemphasis on 'why' and 'how' has underplayed the importance of 'what'.

In SIDH, an organisation based in Mussoorie, Uttarakhand, we have tried to challenge some of these categories and assumptions of modern education. The emphasis is on 'how to think' rather than 'what to think'. Rather than teaching what the Mahatma said, we try to understand why he may have said what he said, for example, why he never ever used the word 'development' in his writings or speeches without first qualifying it. We try and understand the assumptions behind the word 'development'; what is the relationship between non-violence and courage to be able to say no; to be not restricted by categories especially of the man-made law; what is the difference between opposing and non-cooperation/ignoring; what is the difference between sameness and equality; what is the value; what is the difference between *angreziat* and *angrezi*; the difference between respect or trust and its demonstration; what are systems and how they (unknowingly) mould our thinking and actions; what are categories and how they may (unknowingly) influence us; what is the difference between being influenced and being inspired; how we can teach without textbooks by using the local—environmental and cultural—context. Lastly we try to refrain from using 'should' in our schools.

We feel it is extremely important today to challenge the myths and categories created by modernity through education. This is the only way out to pave the path towards real freedom. Our experience is that it is possible to teach these things even to very young children. Once we are able to do this, our young people will learn to feel good about themselves, about who they are. This will unleash self-confidence and creativity among them.

The Tangibles

We need to train on a large scale young people who seem to be floundering, lost, and not knowing what to do. The training must aim to prepare them for both organised—industry and services—and unorganised sectors. It must be localised—say, within a radius of 50 to 80 km—and sensitive to local needs. Industries and services dominant in the area can be surveyed to assess their needs of manpower and skills. The training provided should be aligned with the findings of the surveys. This could well stem large-scale migration as well.

Since such training is in the interest of potential employers, it must be undertaken in collaboration with them and with their active involvement. In fact, the employers could be motivated in many cases to do so on their own. Funds earmarked for corporate social responsibility could be used for such purposes. Some other incentives for both the industry and the youth too could be provided.

Our Industrial Training Institutions (ITI) have failed because there was very little interaction between them and their potential industry clientele to start with. Changes occur continuously and rapidly in the user industry. If it is roped into the design and conduct of training programmes, their curricula will automatically keep pace with these changes. The industry could be motivated to keep the graduates of the training programmes for a trial period (probation). Those who match the criteria for staff and line functions could be retained permanently. This dovetailing of training and employment will give an impetus to the programme as well as young people.

The unorganised sector comprising cottage, tiny and small scale units engaged in handloom and other enterprises such as traditional crafts as well as farming, horticulture, herbs, small units producing processed food items such as poppadams, chips and pickles, among others, also needs to be involved. These activities have been long neglected despite their huge potential. They need some state support. At least hurdles created by the state and its functionaries need to be removed.

Just to give an example, I believe a city of the size of Kolkata has over two lakh pan shops, which, on an average, provide employment to at least three people each, sometimes as much as seven to eight persons, thus engaging about a million in all. They do a daily business of a minimum of ₹3,000 each. Some new shops in Park Street, Victoria and nearby areas of Kolkata may be doing business of ₹30,000-₹35,000 a day. That is not small potatoes. Similarly, street food in India is large business in big cities such as Kolkata, Mumbai as well as small towns, employing millions. By and large, street food is good, hygienic and tasty but seldom gets any support or respect; on the contrary, it suffers hardship and disrespect at the hands of the State authorities, especially the police and municipal bodies. We need a policy to make life a little easier for them and to give them their deserved respect and dignity. Only then can the youth be motivated to look in that direction.

In this age of automation and digitisation, we cannot rely solely on large or medium scale industry and service organisations to provide livelihood to all the youth. Job opportunities will keep shrinking in larger industrial activity. Job creation potential is inversely proportional to the size of investment. The micro, cottage and small enterprises employ more people per unit of investment as compared to larger firms.

Hence these activities need strong impetus. Young people need to be encouraged to become entrepreneurs just as their forefathers were. India used to produce between a quarter and a third of the global manufacturing output. Our craftsmen, who were masters of their production, produced steel, cotton, brass, copper, and stone wares, but not in factories. It is their progeny is what we are concerned about today. They have no respect for the craft in which their forefathers excelled. That respect needs to be restored by giving them confidence and dignity.

Lastly we need to create space for the ordinary. The race for all to become number one is taking us nowhere. Everyone cannot be first in a (mad) race. India gained superiority because the ordinary was excellent and not because a few excelled. The ordinary here was exalted and had a beautiful coexistence with values. We were not competing with each other all the time. So let us now create space for the ordinary. Spaces where youth can meet, play and discuss—ordinary spaces, playgrounds—are shrinking. Let us recreate them and let the youth breathe freely.

2

ADITI GUPTA and AJAY MEHTA

Youth Policy

Dialogue with Youth

Policy is not the Answer

Today, most public intellectuals are focussing on advising the government on how to solve manifold societal problems. Many good policies have been developed through in-depth understanding of the problems, and have helped tackle them to a large extent. For example, banning dowry has led to women's empowerment. Yet, unfortunately, dowry cases continue to occur, though perhaps in small numbers. The ban has caused new forms of problems to emerge, such as false cases and extortion of the groom's family.

While not undermining the value of policy, it is important to note that perhaps more often than not, experts forget real people as they get preoccupied with policy. True change materialises among ordinary people through day-to-day decisions of responsible organisations and individuals, regardless of the policy structure around them.

Democracy is a culture, and not merely the act of selecting a leader and demanding beneficial policies. Real democracy, according to Gandhiji, focuses on change among common people, and they consider themselves responsible for social uplift. As we contemplate and demand policy changes, we increasingly ignore actions of individuals, small organisations and communities.

Two experiences from the epic 85 year-journey of Vidya Bhawan, Udaipur, in the field of education, one generic and the other individual, help elaborate this hypothesis. The first is Vidya Bhawan's identity crisis starting in the 1970s, after a long period of revolutionary work in education. The second concerns Mona, a class

XI student of one of Vidya Bhawan schools, who committed suicide this year.

Vidya Bhawan Crisis: Forgetting the Real People

Dr Mohan Sinha Mehta established Vidya Bhawan in 1931. He was inspired by the Boy Scouts movement as also by Gandhi and Tagore, who believed education to be the agent of societal and individual transformation. Vidya Bhawan was strongly motivated by the ideas accompanying India's freedom struggle, of swaraj and inclusion, and the literary and reformation movements that accompanied it. Dr Mehta was driven by the faith that whenever independence came, India would require educated and committed citizens with determination to establish and sustain democracy.

The Vidya Bhawan Senior Secondary School, Fatehpura, the first institution in the Vidya Bhawan family, was revolutionary in many respects. It was among the first Indian co-educational schools. It emphasised extra-curricular activities and equal treatment of students from various religions, castes and classes. It was the first school in Rajasthan to prescribe a uniform for students to counter visible marks of religious, class and other differences. It encouraged students to participate in activities involving social justice, national and local culture, and ecological awareness. Parents were involved as never before and learnt that schools are not just about literacy but overall development of the child. Positive discipline instead of physical punishment may be a standard practice today, but it was radical in those times. Vidya Bhawan forbade any kind of physical punishment to children.

There was an air of freedom with active encouragement of debate, discussion and cultural programmes. Saturday afternoons were devoted to them. The student union was allocated seven days a year when, due to pleasant weather (monsoon etc.), it could decide to engage in outdoor activities in place of regular classes.

For about its first decade, Vidya Bhawan practised no grading in its classrooms. Thereafter, grading did start, but was limited to naming only the first three positions. The rest were put in two categories, pass or fail. Every effort was made not to fail anyone with a system of re-examination, supplementary homework etc. in place. In the playing fields, everybody had an equal opportunity to participate. The guiding principle was that the joy of playing came not from winning but from the very act of playing. Students were offered a variety of craft activities (carpentry, leather work etc.) as well as gardening.

Graduates of the school in those times grew up to be dynamic, idealistic individuals, who were not only highly successful in their chosen fields, but were also actively involved in societal development. Many of the later alumni continue to be active in issues concerning the school today.

As Vidya Bhawan's expertise in education grew, newer institutions were added to further benefit from it. Teacher training and vocational training schools were started, which were also revolutionary ideas at that time. Vidya Bhawan started a handicrafts teacher training centre in the 1940s encompassing carpentry, leather work, weaving and sewing and papier mache. Not many institutions then possessed comparable innovative educational records, physical assets and unwavering social and ecological commitment.

This initial glory phase lasted about four decades. The rather sudden and rapid expansion of Vidya Bhawan institutions led to a dilution of its idealism and capacity for innovation in some ways. Vidya Bhawan got more and more involved with the government, and acquiesced to becoming a part of it. The government was paying a large part of teachers' salaries. Many Vidya Bhawan associates were strongly influenced by the government.

In 1978, the Vidya Bhawan founder and its then President, Dr Mehta, came under a lot of pressure from the government and its champions within Vidya Bhawan to reinstate a particular teacher who was clearly a derelict, but possessed influence. When he did not give in to the pressure, the government stopped Vidya Bhawan's grant-in-aid. A vocal section of the staff was mobilised to oust him. They succeeded; Dr Mehta resigned.

After this ouster, the Vidya Bhawan culture became one of conforming to the power centres. The new management was more accommodative of pressures. A dilution of the mission and values of Vidya Bhawan ensued. Its progressive features were forgotten, students' results declined and staff morale was affected by factionalism. Teachers saw themselves as civil servants and administrators, accountable in their duties not to students and their parents but to state functionaries and politicians. The student-teacher relationship was no longer defined by democratic principles, mutual respect and care. Education became a mere formality, and stopped being about character-building and social service. The hollow goals of education, which can be seen in so many other educational institutions today, became institutionalised in Vidya Bhawan as well.

Fortunately, after 20 years of this decline, a group of Vidya Bhawan alumni, imbued with its original philosophy, came together to revive its values. A Vidya Bhawan alumnus was elected President in 1994. He embarked on the task of restoration of its progressive educational traditions. The period that followed was of enormous work and creativity. There was a welcome flowering of new domains of enquiry and new institutions came up. However, even as Vidya Bhawan showed renewed vitality, it could not wholly break free of its acquiescing-to-power mindset. This was due to the fact that almost a third of its staff was still on assured state salaries without any rigorous systems of accountability in place. A new power struggle had begun, in which a few teachers were on better government salaries, and others were not. In the process, the ordinary student continued to remain neglected to a great extent, even as Vidya Bhawan was on its way to renewing its foundational values. This regime also ended finally in 2011, when Rajasthan Government withdrew all its funds.

Vidya Bhawan is now recovering from these dynamics, and is gradually attaining full autonomy. This autonomy comes along with a responsibility towards the student, and teachers, and has bearing on its day-to-day decisions. Many internal leaders understand the goals Vidya Bhawan has set for itself and are taking numerous constructive steps towards rebuilding creative engagement with students and a strong value system. This is, however, a slow process and involves considered decisions and breaking away from the contemporary form of education. The institutions are attempting to strike a delicate balance between being attractive to parents and students by producing academic results and other forms of popularly accepted accomplishments, and remaining strongly committed to its core values, which sometimes may appear outlandish to many. Required spaces for more discussion and talk about modern day dilemmas concerning students are slowly emerging, instead of being ignored in the hustle for competition, or focus on policy.

Mona: A Death Foretold

Mona, a class XI student in one of the Vidya Bhawan schools, committed suicide earlier this year. She was known to be involved romantically with a boy in the school, from a different caste. Her brother, Rakesh, assuming the responsibility of the family's honour, beat her up and verbally abused her, which eventually drove her to poisoning herself.

This tragic incident reflects poorly on what Vidya Bhawan stood for originally, and has failed to follow today. The original Vidya Bhawan took very seriously the task of overcoming caste, class and religious prejudices. It was one of the first co-ed schools, and focussed on equitable gender relations. Above all, it made sure that non-violence as an important value was taught and practiced as well. It followed a group approach, in which teachers spent unstructured time with students, aimed at building a relationship with them. In this time, the students also opened up, and talked about things that troubled them. If that system were still functioning, Mona's distress could possibly have been dealt with early on. Earlier, teachers also tried to build relationships with the students' parents, and involved them in discussions regarding their wards. They were mindful of the possibilities of stresses and attempted to alleviate them through dialogue and close interaction. The student-teachers bond was not based on hierarchy and power, but on sharing and mutual respect. Students learnt self-governance and co-operation, as opposed to winning through violence or competition.

These deep engagements got weaker and hollower as power struggle engulfed Vidya Bhawan. In the pursuit of making an impact on policy, students such as Mona and Rakesh, and their need for meaningful, value-based engagements were forgotten. Over the years, the Vidya Bhawan leadership lost sight of the deeper purposes of education, which is to build a fair society through education. It was busy debating questions about sustainability that were doubtless important, but the centre of its preoccupation should have been real people such as Mona and Rakesh. The institution was not geared to respect Mona's freedom to like someone of her choice regardless of caste, of understanding Rakesh's warped sense of honour and enable its teachers to anticipate such dilemmas of their wards in order to help them.

Going Forward

Understanding these pathologies within and outside Vidya Bhawan can help it devise a better plan for the future of the youth. State policy is important, but the roles of civil society, individuals and communities are even more important. Teachers and students need to be brought together and enabled to build relationships based on mutual trust and respect. Teachers need to be motivated to devote their energies to students and their environment, in place of power struggles. Experts must be tasked to focus on creating conducive conditions at the ground level of individuals, instead of seeking only generalised solutions.

Given that the societal paradigms are continuously changing, the need to establish a culture of discussion and debate, about which values should be preserved and which should be let go of, cannot be overemphasised. There will always be generation gaps between the youth on one side and their parents and teachers on the other. This gap needs to be constantly bridged, by respecting the youth, their rights, including the right to privacy, and involving them in discussion.

Schools and colleges must provide regular forums to contemplate the various dilemmas that come up while dealing with youth, which are not given much thought and attention today. They are either quickly resolved based on individual value systems, such as some teachers considering physical punishment to be the appropriate disciplining method, or are ignored because of their complexity and a perceived lack of time. These are the concerns that can help each individual and a society determine its values. Incidents like Mona's death are usually preceded by a number of such dilemmas, which, when ignored, could lead to tragedy. Maybe some teachers did notice something going on with Mona, or maybe they were aware of Rakesh's actions. They probably faced many quandaries, arising out of their concern for Mona, on how to approach this issue. But since these issues were not given space and time, they were ignored, or wrongly dealt with.

We need to teach our youth to take responsibility of change within their lives, and their communities. We need to set examples for these through action on the ground. By concentrating on change from top down, we may be unwittingly giving this message to our youth that the locus of change lies outside them, among the more powerful. The government cannot take care of students like Mona. Saving her was the task of her family, teachers, friends and community. They should have had the means to understand her and act in a non-violent manner to resolve or accept differences.

To conclude, our leaders in education and youth development should be preoccupied with understanding the world of students like Mona and Rakesh. Our education system needs to be reoriented away from the state and expert level, to be taken forward on the basis of an abiding commitment to the youth, and a culture of discussion and consensus at the individual level. Our youth needs to be taught the true definition of civilisation, as enunciated by Gandhiji: a space where people express their ethical responsibility towards themselves and their communities and act accordingly.

3

PRABHAT PANKAJ

Youth Policy for Young India

Background and Overview

India as a country is turning old while Indians are becoming younger. This unique phenomenon has opened a window, especially at an opportune time when Indian economy is poised to take-off and the world has started looking at India with hope and admiration. At this juncture, India needs to take proactive steps towards assimilating its youth into mainstream development while ensuring that the development benefits youth in their entirety. For this to happen, two parallel processes need to work in tandem and need to be taken as guiding principles of any policy reform India would be looking for:

i. *Inclusiveness of youth in development process*: There must be a youth coefficient in policy process. In a country with more than 50 per cent of young population, it would not make any sense if we do not assimilate the views of youth in policy making as an important stakeholder. Youth must be asked what and how they want the policy and development in general to deliver. Youth must form part of both policy making and development process.

ii. *Development process in turn must benefit youth*: Policies must ensure that the outcome is focussed on benefitting youth. Evaluation of programmes and policies must consider how many and in what manner they have benefitted the youth of our nation.

India: A Young Nation @70

Though various estimates of population distribution, projection, and growth of young population differ a bit, most of them concur that India's young population in the age group 15-24 would see a bulge. This qualifies India as a young nation on the world map. Table 3.1 compares the United Nations (UN) population estimates to those of India.

Table 3.1

Average Annual Increment in Youth Population (15-24), in Million

	UN Population Database			*Registrar General of India*		
	Total	*Male*	*Female*	*Total*	*Male*	*Female*
2001-2006	4.0	2.0	2.0	5.4	3.0	2.4
2006-2011	2.7	1.3	1.4	3.5	1.7	1.9
2011-2016	1.3	0.6	0.7	(0.2)	(0.3)	0.1
2016-2021	0.2	0.1	0.2	(1.9)	(0.8)	(1.1)
2021-2026	0.1	(0.1)	0.1	(1.1)	(.3)	(0.8)

Source: Adapted from Chandrasekhar, C.P. Jayati Ghosh, Anamitra Roy Choudhury (2006). "The 'Demographic Dividend' and Young India's Economic Future", *Economic and Political Weekly*: 5058, 9 December.

The UN estimates show the youth population (15-24 age group) bulge will start declining only by 2025 while the Indian estimates suggest that this may set in a little earlier. The demographic dividend is largely seen as a consequence of a particular phase of demographic transition, when a nation experiences a decline in birth rate and perceptibly low mortality rate along with improvements in the life expectancy. Taken together, these changes in the age distribution lead to a larger working age population in comparison to dependent population.

Table 3.2 provides estimates of dependency ratios in India since the year 2000.

India is likely to witness this transition in the estimated dependency ratio of non-working population to the working age population declining from 0.60 in 2001 to 0.48 in 2025. In 2021, about 64 per cent of India's population will be in the working age group, with 63.5 million new entrants in 2011-2016. Unlike India, most major economies of the world including China, Western Europe, and North America will all see an increase in the dependency ratio. By 2025, India's average age is estimated to be around 25, while it will be 40+ in major developed countries. This means that as major economies of the world will tend to lose productivity due to the ageing workforce, India will have a unique window of opportunity called the demographic dividend for at least the next 20 years.

Table 3.2

Trends in the Dependency Ratios in India

(in %)

Year	*Dependency Ratio*	*Child Dependency Ratio*	*Old-Age Dependency Ratio*
2000	64	56	8
2005	60	51	8
2025	48	36	12
2050	50	27	22

Source: Same as Table 3.1.

Education for Youth: Not Keeping Pace with Time

The answer to the age-old question, why education, seems to have undergone a sea change. The early belief that education makes you a better human being with refined social traits got eroded in the wake of the productivity debate. Examples from everywhere suggest that education does not always make you a better human being with a high level of sensibility towards the society, as reflected in the growth of white-collar crime. Later on, even the so-called productivity paradigm was questioned: an educated person is not always demonstrably more productive. The examination system has been questioned in the absence of a correlation between productivity and credentials earned. The growing market demand for hands-on competence led to the job-access paradigm. This provided an entry window to the private sector into education with the responsibility of converting the educated into the employable. This must be seen in the context of our situation, where only 7 to 8 per cent of the school-leavers at the 10+2 (pre-university) stage manage to enter the 18,000 colleges and universities, another 1 to 2 per cent secure some kind of a job, and the rest are either unemployed or looking for some employable skills.

About 26 million people are added to our education system which has a dismal infrastructure. Educational crowding out is a reality. The supposedly educated are placed out of context and they find it difficult to join mainstream. The only way to bring them back to system is to make education system responsive to the needs of market for employable skills and an outward orientation.

Big Employability Gap: Degrees are Credentials without Value

The NASSCOM Report 2010-11, found only 25 per cent of Indian engineering graduates to be employable. Currently, 50,000 engineering graduates are produced every year which is likely to exceed 1 million in 2015-2020. The situation is even more challenging for management graduates and graduates of other streams. Entrance examinations for IITs, IIMs, and other prestigious institutions attract about 600,000 applicants every year. The business of pre-coaching thus amounts to ₹12,000 crore a year at an average expenditure of ₹2 lakh for each candidate. About 6,000 seats are available in these premier institutes. Therefore, a huge sum is spent with a probability of success of 1 per cent. Indeed people are paying for values, which are simply not delivered by our educational institutions. Their degrees are just credentials without value. It should be startling to note that about 300 million people in the age group 18-50 will be looking for employable skills while the market will be able to cater to less than 10 per cent.

School Education: Three Fold Problems

Schools are at the base of our education system. They have a three fold problem:

i. Access to schooling (bringing children to schools);
ii. Drop-outs (keeping children in school); and
iii. Learning gaps (making children learn in school).

This is not just an infrastructure gap, but a huge service delivery gap as well, which is a systemic and governance problem. The gross enrolment ratio in the 11-13 age group is lower than 6-10 age group, indicating drop-outs. The teacher-classroom ratio, currently 74 per cent, is declining while the number of schools, colleges, and universities has increased several-fold. A major cause of concern is that the percentage of children in class 5 able to read a standard

2 level text has declined from 54 per cent in 2010 to 47 per cent in 2013. The percentage of children able to solve simple 2-digit subtraction problems fell from 39 in 2009 to 26 in 2013. Children's attendance in class 1 to 5 declined marginally from 73 per cent in 2010 to 71 per cent in 2013 in rural primary schools.

Mass Spread of Higher Education: Surge in First Generation Learners

There has been a surge in gross enrolment ratio in higher education. Most of it seems to be coming from Tier-2 and Tier-3 cities. This indicates that India is in line with the global trend of mass spread of higher education. This requires expansion of capacity and enlarging supply of higher education. The entry of private institutions has driven capacity-building and possibly, quality improvement. This has also reduced the pressure on public institutions and passed the cost of education on to students and parents. Private institutions could yet play a bigger role; however, not many of them figure in international rankings. This is a matter of serious concern, which reflects on the relatively poorer attention to quality and quality assurance framework in these institutions.

It has a sociological underpinning as well. A large number of entrants to higher education in pursuit of jobs are from Tier-2 and Tier-3 cities. Most of them are first generation learners with no experience of learning at home. This affects their learning style and poses a challenge of a different nature. A student-centric education system with a learning-centric approach is likely to meet those challenges better.

Globalisation and Technology: Need Faster Adaptation and Assimilation

Yet another strong factor guiding the youth in general and education in particular in India is the imperative of globalisation. Today's youth is motivated by global aspirations. As the economy and businesses think global, education needs to prepare students who can take up global challenges. Technological developments in this era are creating massive opportunities, but they come with their own challenges. India produces a large number of graduates at cheapest costs in comparison to the US, China, and Europe. It is, however, still not able to attract international students in any significant numbers. The education quality deficit in India is glaring.

Reverse Brain Drain: Why is it not Happening for India?

Today, 70,000 to 90,000 Indian students go abroad every year in search of skills and degrees. In any given year, these 320,000 students in four-year programmes abroad cost the country about USD 9 billion.

Can we better utilise this resource? One way would be to use this money, sufficient to build 40 IIMs or 20 IITs. Given the sheer low cost of education in India, once we become a global hub of education, the student preference could start shifting from North America, Australia, or Singapore to India. That would also allow Indian youth to grow better in a multi-cultural environment. But with the existing huge quality and service delivery deficits, it is unlikely to happen any time soon.

Inclusive Development: Need to Bridge Rural-Urban Gap

A large workforce in India is associated with unorganised sector. Out of the total employment of 459 million in 2004-05, about 57 per cent was found self-employed, 29 per cent as casual labour, and about 14 per cent as regular wage labour. A large proportion, 92 per cent, is in the non-formal sector, while only 8 per cent works in the organised sector. Unorganised workforce exists in both rural and urban area. There is also a large difference in rural and urban work systems, infrastructure, and opportunities for youth.

Female Participation: Yet Another Dampener in Demographic Dividend

The demographic dividend is about participation of young population in workforce. Not many women come out and join the job market or start business of their own, even though they are educated. The low workforce participation rate of 34 per cent for females in India is a major concern. Given that 50 per cent of the bulge in young population will be women and the effective dependency ratio estimated to go up to 1.26 for India by 2030, this state of affairs does not confer any advantage on India. Women who are able to complete school or take a degree from college need to remain in job markets or start something of their own.

Health and Happiness for Youth: Healthy Minds in Healthy Bodies

Indian youth is reported to suffer from anxiety, depression, and psychological disorders. Happiness is missing from their young lives. The worst result of youth despair is suicide. Students committing suicide under pressure of competitive examinations, failing to earn livelihood, or when caught in repressive circumstances is a big blemish on our society. Health and happiness cannot be compromised, if we really want our youth to assume leadership positions.

Mapping Youth Aspirations: Survey Results

Rationale

Youth is the first and the most important stakeholder in the policy about youth. It is important to consult them for two reasons:

i. Policymaking must have stakeholder perspective. This is important for developing an inclusive policy.
ii. Policymakers and the youth belong to two different generations. Understanding the perspective of youth and their aspirations would enable the policy to be broad based, which would be otherwise too narrowly focussed.

Methodology

We contacted 300 young persons through emails, but only to management students currently pursuing a master's programme or recent graduates in jobs. This is a major limitation. Thus, the results may not be representative but, in view of the homogeneity of generation Y in terms of habits, exposure, aspirations, and access they would nevertheless be indicative of the essence of the views of the generation. Only 42 responses, hailing from 12 states, have been gathered and incorporated in the findings within the time limit.

A letter accompanying the email explained the background to the survey, elaborated earlier in this paper. The following four questions were posed:

i. What do you think are the top 5 things the education system should deliver to you?
ii. What do you think are the 5 top priorities of the youth of our nation today?
iii. What do you think should be addressed in the youth policy of our nation?
iv. Please fill in the blank in the sentence below keeping your aspirations from Youth Policy in mind:
We are generation 2025. We do not want............ We want............

Results: Deliverables of the Education System

i. *Practical learning:* Companies nowadays hire freshers with practical knowledge rather than those who have only theoretical knowledge. High marks are important but knowledge without ability to implement the learned skills is of no use.
ii. *Life skills*: The curriculum should provide opportunities to develop life skills such as teamwork, problem solving and enterprise and permit experience in a range of future options. Life skills should be taught through practical activities linked to academic subjects and vocational areas.
iii. *Practicality of reservation*: Reservation is undeniably a need of our society, but why is it benefitting those who have adequate wealth and resources to grow? Reservation should be provided on the basis of standard of living.
iv. *Examinations:* The system should test the practical approach. Presently, students memorise everything and write it in the answer paper. Even the teachers expect students to use bookish language, which gives the students high marks but

low learning. This is not fruitful as memorising and learning are two different things.

v. *Social work*: From the school level itself, students should be given opportunities for social work, which will enable them to know the ground reality and work towards social upliftment.

vi. *Proper counselling:* Industries offer a number of courses and opportunities but students still stick to engineering, medicine, law, or management courses. Proper counselling of students and parents will ensure better future for students through increased job opportunities in the new fields.

vii. *Technology*: Teachers should be trained to use new technology of teaching, including visual learning. Schools and colleges should be technology-enabled with good wi-fi and internet connectivity.

viii. *Games and sports:* Sports bring mental freshness enabling students to better focus on their studies. They should be included in the curriculum.

ix. *More options*: There should be more options to choose from. Many unconventional fields of study, such as cooking, painting, and entrepreneurship, should have professional courses right after high school.

Some Select Quotes from Respondents

Today's youth is confused as well as confident; some are very confident about their career but some are distracted as well.

We do not want to see trial and error methods. We want efficient, effective, and to-the-point communication.

As the boundaries of the nations are vanishing, youth is looking for opportunities inside and outside the country. We don't want to lag behind.

Results: Youth Priorities

i. *Education and skill*: Provide skills and practical knowledge as required by the market.

ii. *Jobs*: Job opportunities for all and also in specialised knowledge domains.
iii. *Freedom of expression*: Platforms and opportunities to speak up and express thoughts freely.
iv. *Money*: We are more materialistic compared to previous generations.
v. *Independence*: We love to be independent.
vi. *Fair competition*: No discrimination please! We need fair and competitive environment, with equal opportunities on the basis of talent.
vii. *Technology*: We need more technology-based systems rather than manual ones.
viii. *Healthy work environment*: Today's youth needs conducive and healthy working environment. Happy employees perform better.
ix. *Right guidance*: We want guidance/mentoring for career growth.
x. *Identity*: Youth looks for identity.
xi. *Social connect*: We would like to repay the society in terms of money, education, charity, employments and so on.
xii. *Pride*: We want to take our country to the position of global leadership and feel proud about it. We want to live with our head held high.
xiii. *Entrepreneurship*: We would be entrepreneurs rather than employees.
xiv. *No corruption*: We hate corruption and we do not want to be a part of it. We would like to work against it. Corruption-free education is one of the greatest need of our nation.
xv. *Be different*: We want to do something different.

Some Select Quotes from Respondents

We do not want things to be forced upon us. Keep us out of divisive politics, we want to take part in fair decision-making systems.

We want to be well-versed in communication skills and also would like to learn how to manage our time.

Those who did MA or MCom are not getting jobs, so it is better to shut these courses and start only professional courses which could help in getting jobs.

Results: Youth Policy Issues

i. *Jobs and skills for youth*: The policy should address the concern of job creation for millions of youth. It should also focus on right to get skilled for the youth.

ii. *Jobs of choice*: Creation of jobs that are youth-centric and interest the youth and also which enhance their skills and help them follow their passions.

iii. *More focussed on Indian value systems*: Indian values should be emphasised to provide right directions to youth.

iv. *Involving youth in decision-making*: Youth policy must advocate involvement of youth in decision-making.

v. *Entrepreneurship*: This is the need of the time and youth must be facilitated to take this course in life.

vi. *Sustainable development*: Create a great workforce that can make a sustainable contribution for the country's development.

vii. *Health and sports*: Youth policy must focus on a strong and healthy generation equipped to take on future challenges through health and sports.

viii. *Social connect*: Promotion of community service should take place through engagement, programmes that give the youth opportunities to contribute to the grass roots development efforts. Promotion of social entrepreneurship is also a way to involve the youth in building the society.

ix. *Youth at risk*: The policy must support youth at risk and create equitable opportunity for all disadvantaged and marginalised youth.

Some Select Quotes from Respondents:

When I was doing my schooling, we never had any counselling session. We definitely need a permanent solution by making it compulsory for every school to have counselling sessions.

The whole idea of education is to enhance overall skill and ability of the individual. We miss the purpose so our education system is making us job-seekers, not job-creators.

In foreign countries, they provide vocational training even after the eighth and the ninth standards. This increases specialisation among students and clarity in their mind about what field they should opt for.

Select Elements of Millennium Friendly Youth Policy

Youth policy must be based on certain principles and values. It must address holistic needs of the young population and be millennium friendly. It should address the physical, social, economic, psychological, and spiritual dimensions of a young person's life. The policy should also be broad-based and all-encompassing. It must aim to integrate various strata, groups, and ethnicity. It should also address youth at risk and its disadvantaged sections.

Values to Follow

The policy must be based on certain values which match the needs of the youth's upliftment and placing them on the centre-stage of national development.

i. *Dignity of youth*: The policy and provisions must reflect and ensure dignity of youth. It should reflect provisions which promote youth identity and make them independent.
ii. *Promoting youth potential*: The policy should focus on promoting the inherent strengths and potential of youth. It should have provisions to make youth independent and self-sufficient.
iii. *Youth empowerment*: Policy provisions should empower youth and raise their confidence level. They should allow youth to contribute meaningfully to their own development and to the development of society.
iv. *Agency of change*: Youth should be viewed as agent of change rather than just a passive recipient of government services.
v. *Forward-looking*: Youth should be taken as the new generation with a forward-looking orientation. The policy must ensure

that the new generation is properly understood and given its due place.

vi *Moral values*: The policy must promote moral and spiritual regeneration of the youth.

vii *Health and happiness*: The policy must support and promote health and happiness of the youth.

Responsibility of Youth

Youth must also be ready to embrace responsibility and be pro-active towards self-development. Youth policy should be about creating conditions for youth's development; however, youth should not only be a receiver of benefits. Youth must act as a responsible citizen. The onus of certain responsibility lies on the youth which they should be ready to embrace and follow.

i. Take up ownership of their own learning and self-development.
ii. Maintain high energy level of energy and strive to perform to full potential.
iii. Work hard.
iv. Follow policy of honesty, kindness, and commitment.
v. Respect diversity and gender. Show love, respect, and care for everything and everybody around them.
vi. Say no to substance use, racism, discrimination, and intolerance.
vii. Promote voluntarism and service to society and nation.
viii. Protect environment and promote cleanliness.
ix. Promote and defend democratic values and participate in its processes.
x. Act as peace agent to curb violence, corruption, and criminality.
xi. Act as role models and strive to take up leadership position in all walks of life.

National Youth Policy 2014: Needs Millennium Friendly Approach

The National Youth Policy 2014 brought out by Ministry of Youth Affairs and Sports, Government of India, spells out 5 objectives of youth policy and 11 priorities associated with it. These objectives and priorities are reproduced as follows:

- *Objective 1*: Create a productive workforce that can make a sustainable contribution to Indian's economic development.
  Priorities: Education, employment and skill development, entrepreneurship
- *Objective 2*: Develop a strong and healthy generation equipped to take up future challenges.
  Priorities: Health and healthy lifestyle, sports.
- *Objective 3*: Instil social values and promote community service to build national ownership.
  Priorities: Promotion of social values, community engagement.
- *Objective 4*: Facilitate participation and civic engagement at all levels of governance.
  Priorities: Participation in politics and governance.
- *Objective 5*: Support youth at risk and create equitable opportunity for all disadvantaged and marginalised youth.
  Priorities: Inclusion and social justice

Select Elements of Millennium Friendly Youth Policy

These objectives and priorities are well-conceived. They, however, still miss the pulse of new generation. Mere enunciation of the right priorities will not help if elements of execution are not millennium-friendly.

Education

i. A serious effort is needed to bridge the service delivery gap in this sector. It is simply not sufficient to bring the children to school and even make them stay in school till the end. It will be more disastrous if students pass out from schools with credentials but fail to live up to their worth.
ii. The number of teachers is definitely a concern but improving the quality of existing teachers is no less important.

Key idea: Happiness must return to the life of the youth. Happiness enhancement workshops can help youth gain positive momentum. Let us start measuring happiness quotient of our society.

Social Engagement

i. Today's youth wants to give back to the society a part of what it received. We must give them a platform and a plan to do so. Giving back to society in terms of services needs to be reinforced.
ii. Social internship and short-term engagement can be made mandatory parts of school and college education.
iii. A massive social engagement programme for youth at national level is needed.

Key idea: Socially engaged youth is a harbinger of change and also of a more satisfying lifestyle.

Mentoring and Counselling

i. A true mentor is like angel in the life of a young person. Our school and college system has failed to provide a genuine system of mentorship. This needs to be rectified.
ii. A psychological counsellor steps in when a system goes wrong. We need to avoid this. A life coach with positive and proactive advice can ensure that the need for psychological counselling is minimised.
iii. Our policy must also address parents and guide them towards positive parenting. A lot of irreversible damage is done at the family level in view of poor handling and counselling.

Key idea: Positive mentoring and life-coaching can work wonders in the life of a youth. Parents as the first life coach need to grow with the child.

Youth at Risk

i. A section of youth suffering from special conditions, such as a physical handicap, HIV-AIDS etc, face social exclusion. The policy must address their concerns and bring them into the mainstream.

ii. Youth from underprivileged sections of the society needs special attention and consideration.
iii. Civic engagement must also bring youth at risk into its fold.

Key idea: We will be losing a great part in demographic dividend, if we fail to engage and strengthen youth at risk.

Youth Consultancy

i. Youth consultancy to map the aspirations, likes, dislikes, and the entire milieu in which youth operates is strongly advocated. This will offer major insights into formulation of right policies.
ii. Youth being the most important stakeholder, youth consultancy will also be an opportunity to incorporate their perspective in the policy.
iii. A policy so made will have greater acceptability and be more effective in implementation.

Key idea: We cannot just have a policy which does not have a buy-in for those for whom it is being made.

Concluding Observations

i. There is a strong cause for adopting stakeholder perspective in youth policy-making. Today's youth wants to be heard. A youth survey is to map their aspiration and views is strongly recommended.
ii. Education delivery systems need overhauling. A major shift in approach from teacher-centric to student-centric needs to be facilitated.
iii. The shift in education delivery systems also calls for a greater use of technology-enabled learning. Rural and urban areas need to be equally equipped as far as technology is concerned.
iv. Skill-building and employability-enhancement need to be mandatory parts of delivery at our schools and colleges. A special emphasis on building non-cognitive skills such as grit, teamwork, optimism, and a growth mindset should be inculcated.

v. The roles of mentors and life-coaches are of paramount significance for guiding youth. We need to ensure positive reinforcement through mentorship and life coaching programmes.
vi. The policy must also address the parents towards positive counselling of children and making them independent decision-makers.
vii. It is time that health and happiness are emphasised in a big way for our youth. It would serve a lot of purpose if a happiness survey is conducted to measure societal and youth happiness.
viii. Social engagement of the youth is a must and a massive programme must be launched at schools and colleges.
ix Special consideration should be given to youth at risk and youth from underprivileged sections of our society.

In the end, this is what our youth opined on being Generation 2025:

> We are generation 2025. We do not want to be just 'Receivers'. We want to be 'Givers'.

4

COMMUTINY and YOUTH COLLECTIVE*

Keep the Change

How to Make Sustainable Long-term Progress on Sticky Social Issues

Context

Change is inevitable they say, but is it? Take the capital of India. The metro system was meant to reduce traffic congestion and pollution. Strong laws against gender violence were supposed to make the city safer. Attracting a lot of industry and corporates to satellite cities in the National Capital Region (NCR) was touted as a sure shot way of creating jobs and reducing inequality.

And yet, Delhi/NCR remain among the five worst polluted cities in the world, with one of the highest traffic congestion rates in any city. Its record on gender violence continues to be abysmal. It is sometimes called the rape capital of the world. As many as 6 rapes and 15 molestations are reported every day and many more go unreported.[1] Unemployment in the NCR region is higher than the national average and has the second highest levels of inequality in the world after Johannesburg in South Africa.

In today's world, we are grappling with myriad social problems ranging from sanitation to intolerance and inequality. In spite of devoting substantial efforts, attention and resources, we have yet to make a sustainable dent in solving these issues. Are we missing a piece of the puzzle?

Take a seemingly easy issue to solve: sanitation. Build enough toilets and we would have made a pretty large impact, goes the

---

* Authored by Arjun Shekhar, Kanika Sinha and Saudamini Pandey.

1. *http://indianexpress.com/article/cities/delhi/2015-average-of-6-rapes-15-molestations-each-day*

handed down wisdom. Under the Nirmal Bharat Abhiyan scheme of the previous government, ₹10,000 per toilet was allocated. The Swachchh Bharat Abhiyan of the present government, underway since 2015, raised it to ₹12,000 per toilet. Nearly 59 lakh toilets have been built from 2008 to 2015.[2] At first, people welcomed the new infrastructure that the government helped build in their homes. Some even took to using them. But many were not able to accept performing an ablution that they deemed to be dirty to them minds within the *sanctum sanctorum* they called home. They went back to their old habits. So, 40 per cent of rural India still defecates in the open despite government-built toilets either at home or in the vicinity. They are typically used for storing grain and shelter goats.[3]

A Different Kind of Change

We at ComMutiny—The Youth Collective (CYC) and PRAVAH have been experimenting with a different approach to social issues for the last 23 years, which seems to indicate a possibility of being able to keep the change, to make it sustainable. We call this a psycho-social approach, a way of changing the world inside out.

PRAVAH works with adolescents (both in school and out of school), youth (in and out of college), with young social entrepreneurs, and with educators and youth facilitators. In 2008, CYC (a PRAVAH and Sir Ratan Tata Trust incubation), was established as a media and policy thinktank with many alumni organisations becoming its first members.

Over the years PRAVAH and CYC have worked with thousands of school students and young people directly on inside out leadership building. The young people undertake a self-to-society journey that helps them reconnect to common spaces even as they discover who they are. As they make change in the world, the world changes them. This is a long term preventive way of keeping the change in the world by building a cadre of socially responsible leaders.

---

2. *https://www.thequint.com/india/2015/08/05/swachh-bharat-who-built-more-toilets-upa-did-better-than-nda*

3. *http://riceinstitute.org/sanitation*

PRAVAH and CYC have spearheaded innumerable youth-led, social action campaigns, addressing issues of discrimination, governance, gender-based violence, and inclusion, among others. Through various initiatives, programmes, events, workshops, CYC, PRAVAH and partners have been able to inspire nearly 1 lakh young leaders in school, out of school, communities, colleges, over the past 20 years of their existence. More than 15 lakh people have been reached extensively and over 400 social change projects and entrepreneurs have been supported.

It is not just the overall numbers that are impressive, but also the impact that these programmes have had on the minds and hearts of young people. While a study revealed tangible effects on performance, career choices and learning orientation, the respondents also showed an improvement in their relationship skills and an ability to influence their immediate circle. Some 85 per cent reported a high level of self-awareness, helping them take inside-out, socially responsible, long-term, preventive decisions. They attributed all this directly to the PRAVAH, CYC and partner facilitated self-to-society journeys they had undertaken.

Are we on the Right Track?

Even as our experiments were in early stages of validating the inside-out leadership building process as a way of changing the world, we decided to test whether the social change theories narrative was itself undergoing a change, since the old ways of impacting social conflicts/issues had failed to sustain a change for the better.

We designed a questionnaire-based social change narrative survey in order to map the kind of interventions or solutions people believed were required to solve major social problems that face the country. The survey was conducted in 15 states with 26,000 respondents. The sample had respondents from different social, gender, caste and age groups.

The methodology was simple. The survey was administered in groups by the CYC member organisations. It consisted of responses to five major social issues facing the youth of this nation—low literacy, religious intolerance, gender discrimination, unemployment, and sanitation. For each issue, the participants had four possible answers. They covered four theories of change or types of interventions needed to solve these social issues at this stage of the nation's progress: changes in legal framework, policy/systems, infrastructure, and mindset respectively. The survey asked participants to allot a total of 3 points across the four intervention options for each issue. Respondents could give all 3 points to a single intervention (say, legal) and 0 to the rest, if they believed overwhelmingly that a particular option was the single most important one needed for solving the problem to the exclusion of all others (say, policy, infrastructure, and mindset). If they felt two interventions (say, infrastructure and legal) would need to be run in tandem, they could distribute their points between them, giving 2 to the one they felt was going to have the stronger effect (say, legal) and 1 (say, infrastructure) to the other, and so on. The team then picked those answers where respondents had shown a clear preference with a score of either 3 or 2. This helped establish primacy of one initiative over the others.

Here is an example of a question and possible responses from the survey to illustrate the above:[4]

In India, 600 million people defecate in open. The new government plans to spend ₹1.26 lakh crore on building more new toilets under the Swachchh Bharat Abhiyan. Previously under Nirmal Bharat Abhiyan, ₹8 crore was spent on building toilets of which 80 per cent unused. In the model village of this programme where from 100 per cent houses with toilets only 1 is actually in use. How will this country make 100 per cent of its citizens stop defecating in the open?

i. Cleanliness policy for every *Gram Sabha*/District ward (Governance/Systemic)

ii. Make new toilets, one toilet per household (Infrastructural)

iii. Make people see the need to/want to use toilets (Psycho-social)

iv. Have a law, fine people defecating outside (Legal)

Respondents' Validation: Psycho-social Approach to Change

The overall analysis of the survey shows that across all the five issues and each of the diverse demographic groups, the psycho-

4. Findings from the entire survey are in Annex.

social approach was rated the most important. Respondents felt that mindset change of the people is the most needed kind of intervention at this stage. This is probably because a lot of work has already been done in the infrastructural, legal and policy/system areas and to make these effective, we now need to change society's old scripts and stereotypes and get young people to take leadership in creating an inside-out change that lasts.

This does not suggest that all legal, policy/system and infrastructural issues have been addressed, which emerged from the survey as well. While mindset change got the highest rank, it was closely followed by legal and systemic interventions. At the same time, the respondents made it abundantly clear, though, that without mindset change, simply making laws and policies and creating infrastructure would not help. This conforms to the general trend in media discussions, too, where commentators recommend psychological interventions to accompany the legal and systemic changes that have been already put in place.

How it all Stacked up: Issue-wise Analysis

The survey questionnaire covered responses for five major social issues currently facing the country. These were: sanitation, gender based violence, communalism, literacy and employment.

Sanitation

Mirroring the general results of the survey, a majority of the respondents believed that psycho-social interventions were most needed to tackle the problem of sanitation. This reflects the feeling that without a change in how people think about sanitation, and unless they feel the need for toilets, there really cannot be any change. Simply building infrastructure, although essential, will not help, as without mindset change, these toilets just remain unused and gradually slip into disrepair. Similarly, legal solutions such as fines are also hard to enforce and will not really lead to a sustainable solution. Both infrastructural and psycho-social interventions are required to tackle the problem of sanitation.

Figure 4.1

Percentage of Highest Ranking Given: Overall

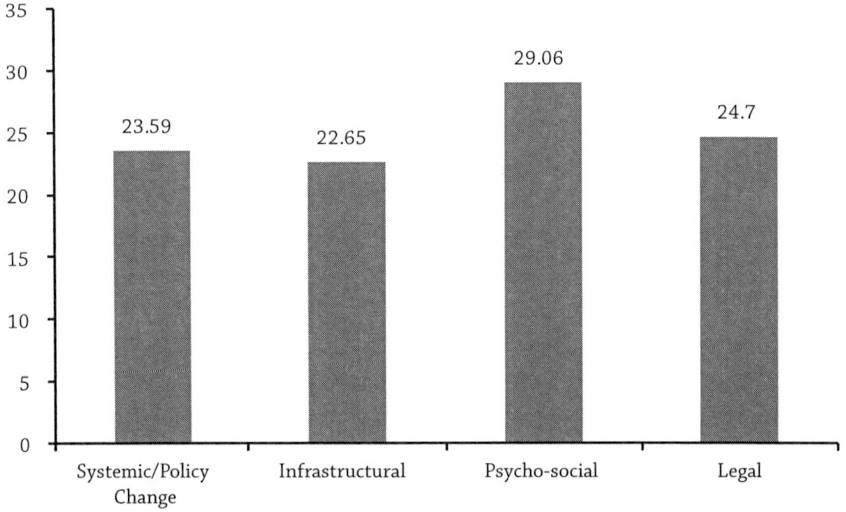

Gender Security

The recognition of the need for mindset change with regard to gender security is hardly surprising. The results of the overall analysis as well as for different categories all point to participants' belief that psycho-social intervention is key to creating gender safety. This is illustrated in the Figure 4.2 where a clear difference is seen between the best and the second best solution for this particular issue. While legal interventions have also been rated as important, people strongly believe that nothing can be effective without working on mindset change.

This need for a psycho-social response to the issue of gender security has also been supported by another experiment that CYC undertook in March 2016. As part of a programme, advertisements were placed in the Delhi Metro. They asked the pertinent question 'Is separate the only way to be safe?' The metro users were asked to share their opinion. A large number of responses mostly pointed towards the need for mindset change.

Figure 4.2

Percentage of Highest Ranking Given: Gender Security

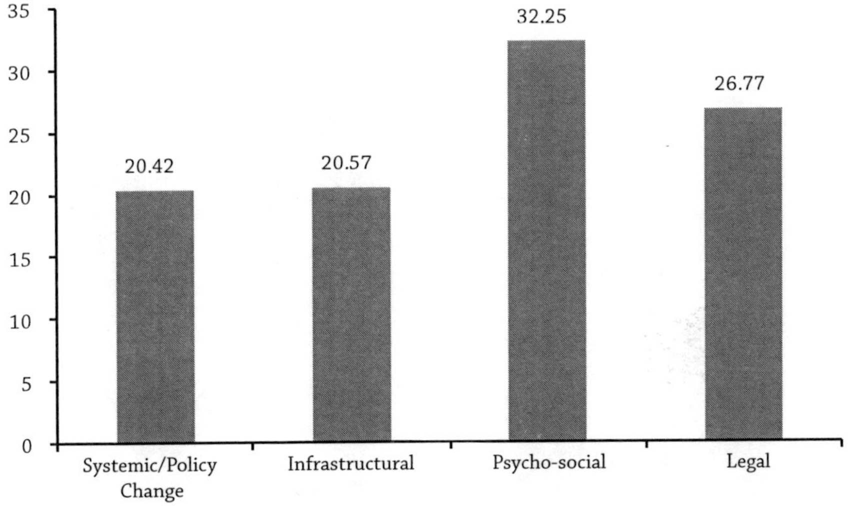

Employability

The issue of employability threw up a mixed bag of responses. While overall mindset change received the highest percentage of responses, the other interventions all followed closely. The demographic breakup and analysis show legal interventions as a very close second followed by systemic solutions. Psycho-social interventions involving shifting the orientation towards learning skills and capacity building as well as encouraging more and more young people to become entrepreneurs (so that they become job-givers rather than job-seekers) are clearly seen as very important. This response, combined with legal interventions in the form of schemes and employment legislations accounts for over 50 per cent of the answers. The responses in favour of legal interventions, particularly from SC, ST and OBC respondents may be linked to the existing reservation and quota systems.

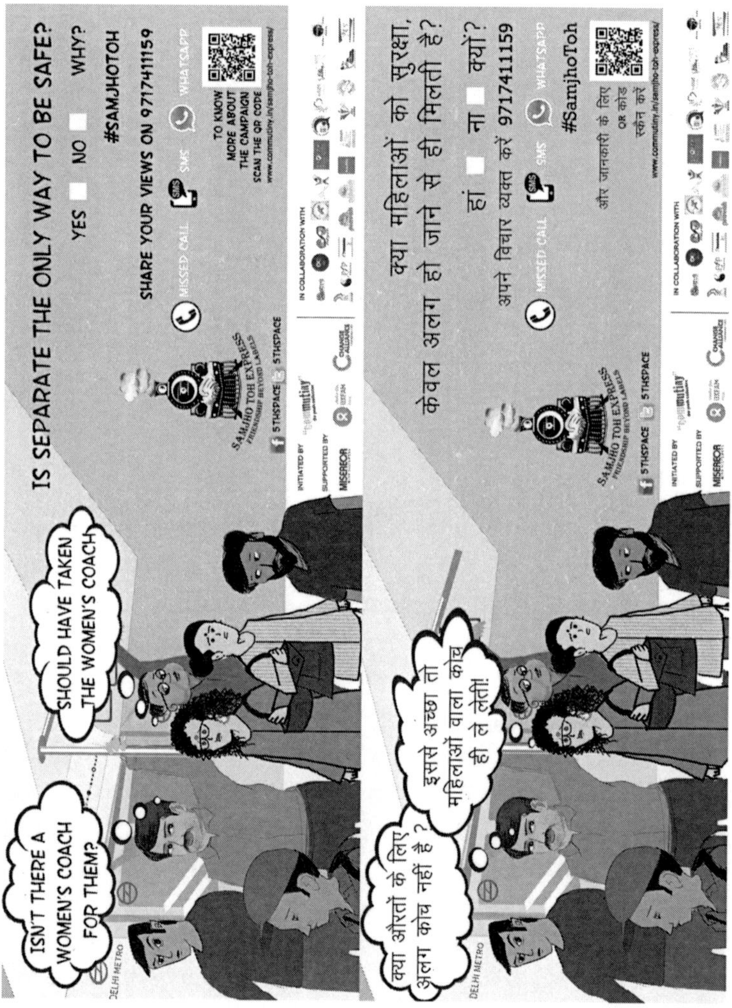
DELHI METRO
ISN'T THERE A WOMEN'S COACH FOR THEM?
SHOULD HAVE TAKEN THE WOMEN'S COACH
IS SEPARATE THE ONLY WAY TO BE SAFE?
YES NO WHY?
#SAMJHOTOH
SHARE YOUR VIEWS ON 9717411159
MISSED CALL
SMS
WHATSAPP
TO KNOW MORE ABOUT THE CAMPAIGN SCAN THE QR CODE
www.commutiny.in/samjho-toh-express/
SAMJHO TOH EXPRESS FRIENDSHIP BEYOND LABELS
5THSPACE 5THSPACE
INITIATED BY
SUPPORTED BY
MISEREOR
IN COLLABORATION WITH
DELHI METRO
क्या औरतों के लिए अलग कोच नहीं है ?
इससे अच्छा तो महिलाओं वाला कोच ही ले लेती!
क्या महिलाओं को सुरक्षा, केवल अलग हो जाने से ही मिलती है?
हां ना क्यों?
अपने विचार व्यक्त करें 9717411159
MISSED CALL
SMS
WHATSAPP
#SamjhoToh
और जानकारी के लिए QR कोड स्कैन करें
www.commutiny.in/samjho-toh-express/
SAMJHO TOH EXPRESS FRIENDSHIP BEYOND LABELS
5THSPACE 5THSPACE
INITIATED BY
SUPPORTED BY
MISEREOR
IN COLLABORATION WITH

Figure 4.3

Percentage of Highest Ranking Given: Employability

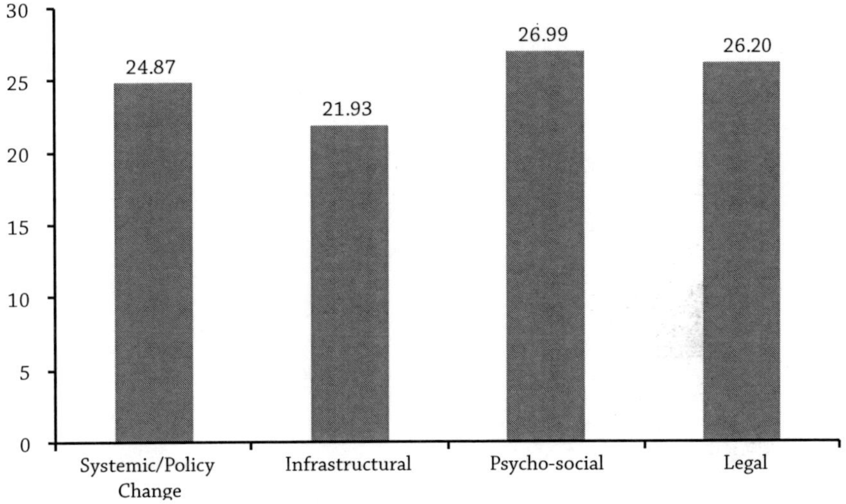

Communalism

Mindset change has overwhelmingly emerged as the most effective intervention to combat communalism as in gender safety. This appears to be a recognition of the fact that a lot of communal incidents are a result of ignorance and stereotypes which are played up and used to fuel fear by irresponsible leaders to raise communal passions. While laws and infrastructure maybe in place to safeguard against such incidents, they cannot truly challenge communal ideologies unless there is serious and focused effort on changing how people think.

Education

Legal solutions to the issue of education and illiteracy in India received the largest percentage of responses according to the survey. Mindset change came a very close second. This could be due to a strong feeling among respondents that the Right to Education Act which has been around for several years needs to be better implemented to solve the problem of enrolment and illiteracy. However, they also recognised that society mindset needs to change simultaneously for the children to remain enrolled and for the parents not to pull their children out of school early and to support their children's aspirations for higher education.

Figure 4.4

Percentage of Highest Ranking Given: Communalism

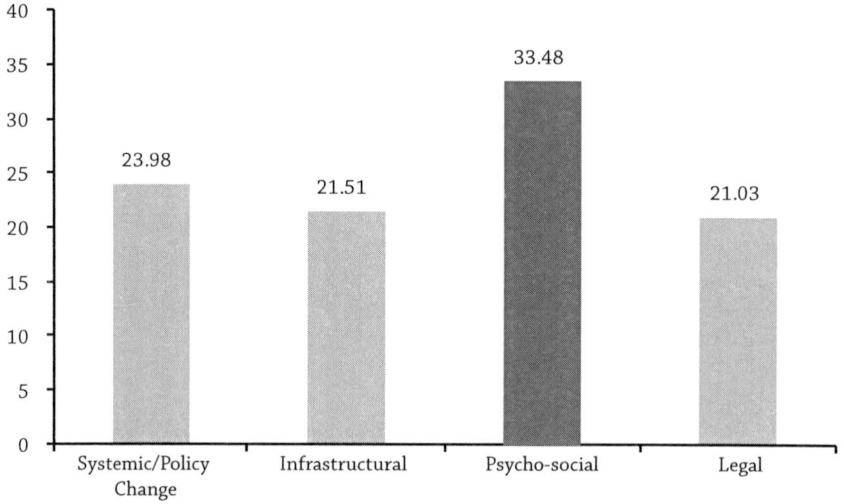

The results of the survey reaffirmed our hypothesis that the problem that still needs to be tackled is that of the mindset. However, almost all the investment by policy-makers, bureaucrats, parents, educators, and media in terms of time, attention, energy and money is devoted to the other options and only a pittance is for the psychological one. In fact, mindset change does not feature in most policy documents and intervention blueprints except as an output of a mass communication strategy. Sustainable change, beyond any doubt, requires a psycho-social intervention.

Conclusion: We Need to be Protective to Keep the Change

You may have heard of the parable of the man who lost his keys. It was night and a sole street lamp was lighting up a small portion of the alley. The man was searching frantically for his key under the lamp. The watchman came along and asked the man what he was doing. "Looking for my keys," the man replied impatiently. "Perhaps I could help", the watchman said. "Sure, any help is welcome." "Where exactly did you lose them?" "I lost them there..." the man pointed to somewhere far away in the dark. The watchman shook his head in bewilderment. "Then why are you looking for them here?" "Because there is no light over there".

Figure 4.5

Percentage of Highest Ranking Given: Education

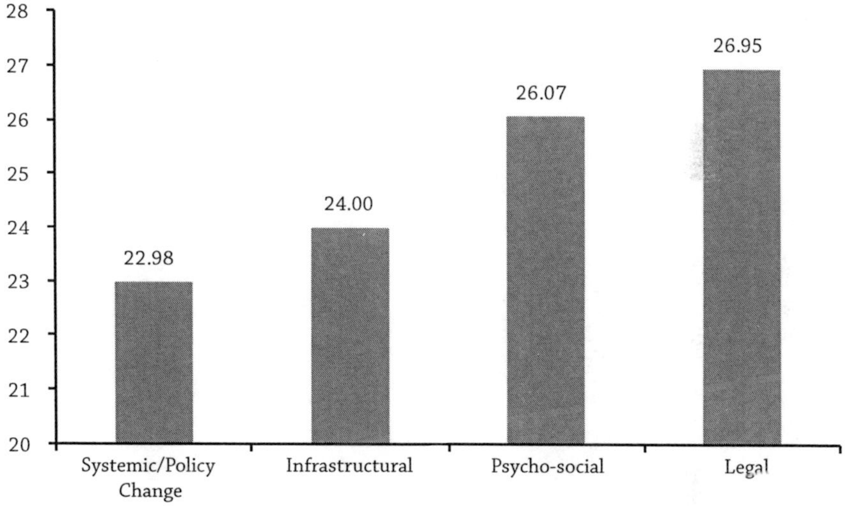

This parable sums up our efforts at keeping the change. We know that to keep the change in society, we need to change people's mindsets. But this psycho-social approach is hard to do. How do you change people's minds at a mass level? Is it even possible to do so at this scale? How long will it take to change this country to change, one individual at a time?

We at PRAVAH/CYC not only believe it can be done, but we have also conducted several pilots with our psycho-social curricula with some pretty impressive results. The best time to intervene is when they are young and impressionable, and the best way is not to hammer change into their minds but to let them see how their minds get made up in the first place. Youth, first and foremost, is an identity formation stage, a time when world views are still being formed and hence the possibility of rescripting their own notions is much higher.

What it requires is for the young person to be able to disengage from the set of beliefs handed down to them and rediscover their authentic selves. An effective, reflective design (reflection with action), with co-created safe and fun spaces is all it takes. We do not need sophisticated facilitators to conduct these sessions, if we have deep, well constructed designs that are more or less self-running or can be co-ordinated by peer educators.

Annex 4

Questionnaire Filled by Respondents

Survey Form

1)	*Personal Details*				
	Name :	Date of Birth (DD/MM/YY):		Gender :	
	Caste :	Religion:		Mobile:	
	Differently-abled: Yes/No			City:	
	E-mail:			State:	
	Educational Qualification:				
	Annual Income (Please tick the appropriate, if applicable)	Up to ₹ 50,000	50 k-1 lakh	1-2 lakh	2 lakh and above

Instructions

This exercise contains a series of five statements. Besides each, are four responses. Select the response that you most agree with. For each of the five statements, you have three points to assign, giving them to one or more of the alternate responses. Here is a typical statement and it has four responses:

Example Statement

According to a Forbes survey, the list of world's top 100 billionaires includes 10 Indians. Also India's top 100 richest people are all billionaires. But inequality in India has doubled in the last 20 years. The top 10 per cent of wage earners now make 12 times more than the bottom 10 per cent, up from a ratio of 6 times in the 1990s. Yet India only devotes 19 per cent of its money and time for charitable causes. How can philanthropy in India be increased?

Responses

i. Make the CSR bill mandatory and ensure penalties are imposed on defaulters.
ii. Create a sense of ownership of common spaces in the minds of the rich and elite.
iii. Create more interface between corporates and NGOs.
iv. Dismantle the processes that foster stashing of black money in India and abroad.

You may assign your three points to indicate your response style as follows:

- If you agree fully with one of the responses (say the second one that begins with—Create a sense) and do not like any of the others, then give all the three points to this selection. In this case, your entry on the Answer sheet will look like the one shown on the right.
- If you like two responses, one a little better than the other, then give two points to your first preference and one point to your second preference. In this case, your entry on the answer sheet will look like the one shown at the right.
- If you like three of the four responses equally well, you can assign one point to each of them. In this case, your entry on the answer sheet will look like the one shown at the right.

To summarise, you must assign three points between each set of four responses. You can follow any of the patterns discussed. Fill in a zero for any response that receives no points. Select the response that you are most likely to make.

Psycho-social

Development boils down to mindset change of individuals towards more humane and compassionate, and development through this lens focuses on the psycho-social development of individuals who come together to form the society. The word psycho-social has been coined to create a combination of the psychological domain with the social domain. In this approach, self development and social development are both given primacy and the crucial interconnection between the two is foregrounded. An investment is made in building of the values, beliefs and identities of individuals in a way that can develop their attitudes, behaviour and mindset, eventually influencing the way in which the society develops on the whole. For example, to address the issue of gender based violence, it is important to revisit the root of the problem and to look at how these identities were constructed and how they create a dynamic of inequality in terms of the patriarchal mindset prevailing in India.

Legal

Let every individual get quick and correct recourse to justice and thus attain a certain standard of life.

The legal narrative of development states that effectively framed laws and their stringent implementation will ensure attainment of social justice and accelerate the process of socio-economic development in the country. These laws may include those on property, commercial law, family law, social welfare policies, taxation policies and criminal law. For example, strict scrutiny is the most stringent standard of judicial review used in USA. Law and Order has been a powerful theme since the 1960s, which has believed that effective deterrence combined with incarceration would act as a strong preventive leading to development.

Exercise

1. In India, 600 million people defecate in open. The new government plans to spend 1.26 lakh crore on building more new toilets under the Swachh Bharat Abhiyan. Previously under Nirmal Bharat Abhiyan, 8 crore was spent on building toilets of which 80 per cent are unused. In the model village of this programme where 100 per cent houses with toilets only 1 is actually in use. How will this country make 100 per cent of its citizens to stop defecating in open?

   a) Cleanliness policy for every *Gram Sabha/* District ward?

   b) Make new toilets, one toilet per household?

   c) Make people see the need to/want to use toilets?

   d) Have a law, fine people defecating outside?

2. After the December 16th Delhi gang rape case there were massive protests and the creation of new and stricter laws. Yet, according to National Crime Records Bureau (NCRB), the number of rapes has increased from 585 in 2012 to 1441 in 2013. India ranks 3rd in world in number of rape cases. How can violence against women be reduced in India?

   a) Have more female cops in public places and ensure proper lighting/Have 'female only' spaces in public transport?

   b) Stricter punishment for offenders/accused?

   c) Have more help lines and redressal forums?

   d) Create spaces for girls and boys to get to know and understand each other from a young age?

3. Only 25 per cent of 7 lakh engineers and 15 per cent of 20 lakh graduates are employable but on the other hand 48 per cent of Indian employers struggle to fill jobs. How do we solve this problem?

   a) Create more employment legislations schemes like MNREGA at the industrial and urban level?

   b) Increase interface between employer and institutes to reduce mismatch between requirement and skills?

   c) Increase the number of skill building and training institutes?

   d) Build the right attitudes amongst youth such as ability to work in a team, willingness to learn, ownership and responsibility?

4. Over the last 8 months, there has been an increase in incidence of communal violence as compared to the previous years. For instances, Muzzafarnagar riots (Hindu and Muslim), Hyderabad (Sikh and Muslim), Kokrajhar, Vadodara and now in Delhi. How can we find a true solution to this problem?
    a) Working on breaking stereotypes about the 'other' communities and work on the communally polarised state of mind today?
    b) Create institutions and forums to address grievances and issues of communal violence?
    c) Political parties should stop fishing in troubled water?
    d) Pass the Anti-communal bill and make it a firm law?
5. Every 3rd child in India is illiterate. India's literacy rate is 74 per cent as compared to world which is 84 per cent. How do we become a fully literate nation?
    a) Increase the number of Government schools in the country?
    b) Take efforts to promote the Right to Education act to make it more popular and ensure it is implemented?
    c) Change the psychology of parents who pull their children out of school early?
    d) Create informal schooling space like *raatrishalas*, informal education centres?

Source: All the data, mentioned in the questions, are from authentic sources. Following are the links:

- *http://timesofindia.indiatimes.com/india/93-women-are-being-raped-in-India-every-day-NCRB-data-show/articleshow/37566815.cms)*
- *http://timesofindia.indiatimes.com/india/Indias-income-inequality-has-doubled-in-20-years/articleshow/11012855.cms*
- *http://www.theguardian.com/news/datablog/2010/sep/08/charitable-giving-country#data*
- *http://en.wikipedia.org/wiki/List_of_countries_by_literacy_rate*
- ILO and NASSCOM.

Infrastructural

Let there be safe spaces and a vigilant state to ensure nothing goes wrong. The context in which society lives plays a huge role in its development. If the context can be created in a way that has preventive measures in place, systems that can keep a check on the implementation of the policies, law and governance, it would further lend to development. For example, China is becoming a surveillance state. In recent years, the government has installed more than 20 million cameras across a country where a decade ago, there weren't many. Today, in Chinese cities, cameras are everywhere: on highways, in public parks, on balconies, in elevators, in taxis even in the stands at sporting events. Officials say the cameras help combat crime and maintain 'social stability'. If there is vigilance and a watch over everything that is done, it builds accountability and transparency which is necessary for development.

Governance/Systemic

Let decision-making become inclusive to provide development to all.

Structures in the societal context often refer to how the power is centred or distributed. If we look at the term 'power' closely, it implies the ability to make decisions for ourselves and others. This narrative believes that the way the structures holds power directly affects the development of the society. Structures could be of many forms right from the micro level of committees in schools to a macro level of political decision-making. For example, *Panchayat Raj* is a system of governance in which *Gram Panchayats* are the basic units of administration. It has 3 levels: *Gram* (village, though it can comprise more than one village), *Janpad* (*taluka* or block) and *Zilla* (district). The Amendment Act of 1992 contains provision for devolution of powers and responsibilities to the *Panchayats* both for the preparation of economic development plans and social justice. This act gave constitutional status to the *Panchayats* and has contributed to the community development in a large way.

5

PRAVAH*

Abilities Beyond Skills

A Curriculum on Life Competencies for Employability

The Setting: India's Youth and the Skilling Challenge

Poised to become one of the youngest nations in the world by 2020, India has to deal with the challenge of gainfully employing 63.5 million young people entering the workforce between 2011 and 2016, according to India's Ministry of Labour and Employment.[1] The youth segment of the population (15-34 age group) is projected to peak at 485 million in 2030.

An impact assessment of the skilling initiatives led by National Skill Development Corporation (NSDC) and partner organisations revealed that a mismatch between what trainees are looking for and what their jobs offer is pushing up the dropout rate.[2] NSDC claims to have trained 55 million workers, of whom only 40 per cent (about 22 million) have been placed over the last five years. When asked where the millions have been placed, and at what pay, the NSDC ex-managing director and CEO, Dilip Chinoy said that they have had problems tracking and monitoring placements because of high attrition rates and constantly changing numbers of migrant workers.

At the other end of the spectrum is the inability of the employers to find the right fit for the job. McKinsey & Company's Education to Employment Survey showed that Indian employers leave around 5 to 10 per cent of positions unfilled; 40 per cent attribute the vacancies to their inability to find candidates with the right skills. To overcome

---

* Authored by Arjun Shekhar, Meenu Venkateswaran, Meghamala Sengupta and Ritikaa Khuunah.

1. *www.technoserve.org/blogs/investing-in-skill-youth-development*

2. *http://www.moneycontrol.com/news/economy/the-way-forward-for-india%60s-skilling-programs*

this gap, surveyed employers spent a substantial amount, offering new hires an average of roughly 30 days training in their first year, compared to an average of 21 days by global companies.[3]

Going Beyond Technical Skills Training

In response to some of the above-mentioned challenges, the livelihoods discourse in the last few years has now widened and most vocational training initiatives include a life skills component in addition to technical skills on mobile/TV repair, electricals, plumbing, tailoring/stitching, and beauty treatment/hair dressing. Currently these include limited skills such as grooming, interviewing, communication, presentation and customer orientation. However, the disconcerting part of this trend is to think of life skills as a subject to be taught within the four walls of a classroom, rather than learnt through facilitated real world experiences.

Given that employability refers to the knowledge, skills, attitudes and behaviour, one needs to get work, stay in work and do one's job well, it follows that employability programmes should address other key needs that employers expect to meet from their staff. It is fairly obvious that employers will look for people who, in addition to technical skills, have the requisite competencies for assuming responsibility, learning, conflict resolution, problem-solving, effective communication, decision-making, leadership and teamwork. It is these competencies that enable a person to perform well and contribute effectively to the employing organisation.

It is our contention that young people cutting across diversities of class, caste, religion, region, geography, and gender are not just seeking a livelihood but looking to live meaningful productive lives, of which a fulfilling career is a key aspect. A fulfilling career enables a young person to discover his/her full potential, grow professionally and develop as a human being, to contribute more effectively to the work community s/he is a part of and to perform well.

---

3. *http://www.msdf.org/blog/2014/04/nsdm-500m-indian-youth-need-new-job-skills-can-indias-entrepreneurs-help/*

There is thus an urgent need to expand the scope of livelihoods programmes to enhance employability, and measure their success not merely in terms of numbers placed, but also in terms of placements sustained, how individuals have grown in their chosen jobs/careers over time and how satisfied they are with their overall quality of life. This would surely be impacted positively if careers (whether as an employee or as an entrepreneur) are aligned to individual aspirations which in turn would impact the young person's ability to choose the right livelihood options, sustain them and perform well.

There is also a scope of vocational institutes/skilling agencies to help nurture a sense of social responsibility among the youth, while investing in skilling education. The youth today do have a social/community dream. It is for us to tap into that need and create curricula that result in socially responsible leaders rather than mere workers. Thus sessions on gender issues, health and well-being, safe and responsible behaviour, hygiene, appreciating differences, stereotypes, win-win strategies, taking full responsibility and comprehending social narratives can be built into the curriculum. If we teach that workplaces are respectful to various differences of caste, gender and religion and each is motivated to contribute to their communities in some way, we are not only helping build a better India, but also responding to the whole person, to his/her needs of physical and financial safety, love and belongingness, self-respect, learning and growth.

Our Response: Abilities Beyond Skills (ABS) Programme

Recognising that current employability programmes do not address the mismatch between employer expectations and potential employee needs, we at PRAVAH are in the process of developing an alternative youth-centric curriculum and offer it to government (Industrial Training Institutes, polytechnics) and private players (Empower Pragati, Centum etc.) in the employability space. It is being developed in partnership with the United Nations Population Fund (UNFPA) and ComMutiny-The Youth Collective. It aims to build abilities/life competencies in the youth being trained at vocational centres. This curriculum can be run alongside the technical training, or can be incorporated into the ongoing vocational training.

Curriculum Goals

- Bridge the gap between expectations of potential employers and employees.
- Equip potential employees with flexible, congruent wholesome leadership values, attitudes, behaviours and decision-making capacities.

Curriculum Overview

The ABS is a 70-80 hour life competencies curriculum. It is envisaged to be rolled out in parallel to the domain curriculum, or can be integrated into the ongoing vocational training. The curriculum can be run with any domain (be it mobile repairing, construction, workers training, beauty and wellness, facilities management, computers etc). The highlights of the curriculum are:

i. *Values, attitudes and behaviours*: This is the core of the curriculum. Sessions are designed to help build meta-capacities in potential employees including aspiration-building, ownership, ability to learn, empathy and creating and interpreting reality. These sessions help potential employees to analyse their needs, build their aspirations, identify the values and attitudes behind their patterns that are stopping them and inspire them to put effort to strengthen their capacities using simple tools.
ii. *Effective decision-making and behaviours*: These are input sessions that help make the potential employee an efficient, effective, happy and desired one by the employer. The sessions are on enhancing productivity, goal setting, project management, decision-making, discipline, customer orientation, empathy, health and well-being, positive relationships, handling cultural transitions, resolving conflicts, teamwork, wholesome leadership skills, and congruence between the inside and the outside.

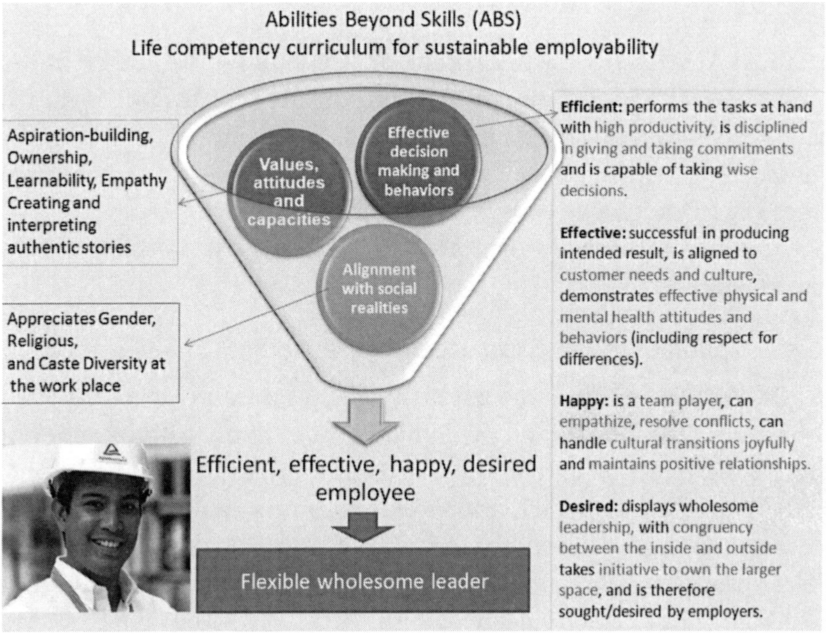

iii. *Alignment to social realities*: The curriculum takes the potential employees a step further and helps to build a socially responsible perspective in them such that they appreciate and respect diversity including gender, caste etc. Thus the effort is to build an agency in the young people/ potential employees such that they can lead self-directed lives and are able to respond to emerging needs of a changed environment.

Experiential Methodology

Another unique aspect of the curriculum is that it moves away from lecture-based pedagogy and instead uses experiential methods. This involves creating experiences within the classroom where potential employees draw on their real life experiences to understand and relate to the topic of the session and learn new frameworks and content. Role-plays, simulations, story-telling, videos, group work, self-assessment, simple inventories and action projects are some of the methods used.

Trained Facilitators

PRAVAH has been in the field of life-skill education for more than 20 years. One of our primary strengths is a group of trained facilitators who are experts in and youth development. Training the technical/vocational agency trainers to roll out the ABS curriculum effectively through five days of input training followed by an optional coaching/handholding for the next three months is a distinguishing feature we offer.

Customisation of the ABS Curriculum for Different Domains

The ABS curriculum is currently 75-80 hours. It is so designed to be customised for different domains. In case the total number of hours is limited, the core module of 20 hours can be run. Additional modules of 20 hours each and extended hours can be selected and customised, based on the need of the potential employees. For effective output, we suggest that the life competency curriculum is 35-40 per cent of the total curriculum.

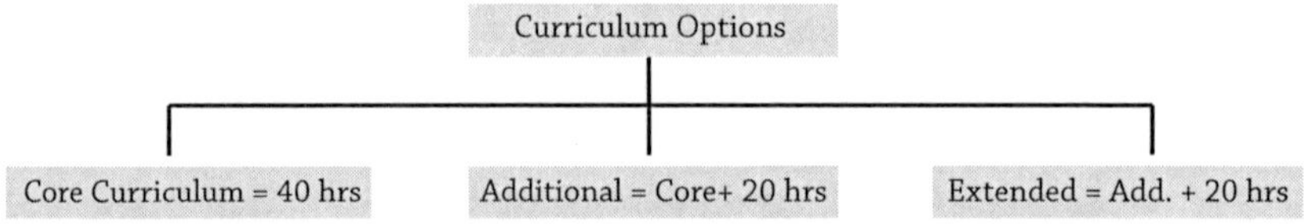

Implementation Strategy and Plans

Our implementing strategy is to work with skilling agencies (government, private, corporate social responsibility foundations). We provide them a robust life competencies curriculum which they can run along with their domain curriculum. We also offer training support to the trainers of the skilling agencies so that they can effectively run the ABS curriculum on ground. The implementation model involves several steps:

Step 1: Partnership with a technical partner: A partner with expertise on domain training and on ground presence of trainers and mobilisers is selected. This partner is responsible for technical/domain curriculum design and development, mobilisation of potential employees, and rolling out the value-added curriculum.

Step 2: Curriculum design and development: We recommend that the ABS core curriculum framework is customised to the needs of specific domain training and audience before being rolled out. This stage also includes design and development of the technical curriculum by technical partner, if not already in existence. PRAVAH provides input into the technical curriculum to exploit possible synergies. The two curricula together are referred to us as the value-added curriculum (technical + life competencies).

Step 3: Training of Trainers (TOT): A four-month journey with 15-20 master trainers of the technical partner by PRAVAH to train and handhold them, to roll out the life competencies curriculum is involved. The journey starts with the selection of master trainers by PRAVAH and technical partner, design of TOT and training of the master trainers by PRAVAH facilitators on the life competencies curriculum.

This step also includes roll out of the value added curriculum to potential employees by master trainers of the technical partner. As the master trainers roll out the curriculum, PRAVAH facilitators observe the trainers on ground and coach them to deal with any challenges to do the same. Technical partners are responsible for project management. In month 4, there is also a refresher workshop of two days planned so that the master trainers can share their learning, celebrate each other and receive inputs for common challenges.

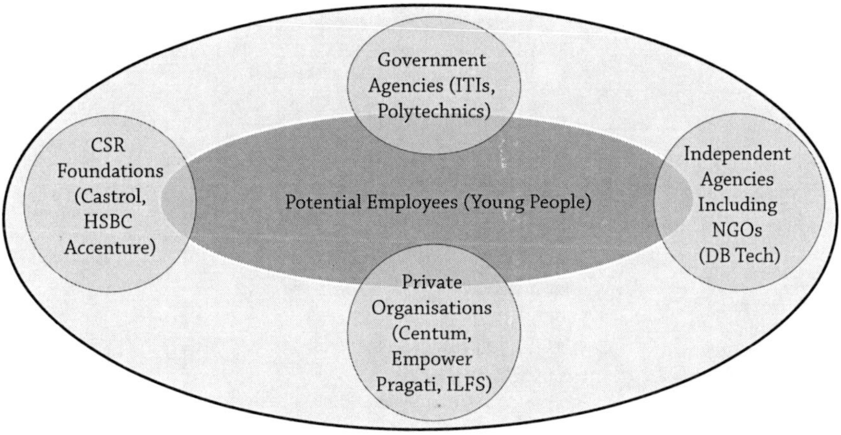

Step 4: Evaluation of this phase and plan for the next phase: The relevant agencies decide the parameters for evaluation at the beginning of the project, based on which tools for evaluation are designed, if required, in the design phase. The experience of this phase helps guide the concerned agencies to decide the way forward.

Piloting the Curriculum

We hosted a stakeholder consultation in June 2015 in partnership with UNFPA to discuss the key challenges in the skilling sector and present the ABS curriculum framework to receive inputs and feedback. Representatives, 29 in all, from corporate, government, foundations and NGOs participated at the consultation. Participating organisations, which included Castrol, BP, Maruti, PwC, Don Bosco, NIIT Foundation and Centum, received the ABS curriculum framework very well. Integrating life competencies in the technical training was seen as a necessity for the skilling sector at the consultation, along with investing in training of trainers to handle the curriculum effectively. We are now in the process of piloting the curriculum with various skilling organisations.

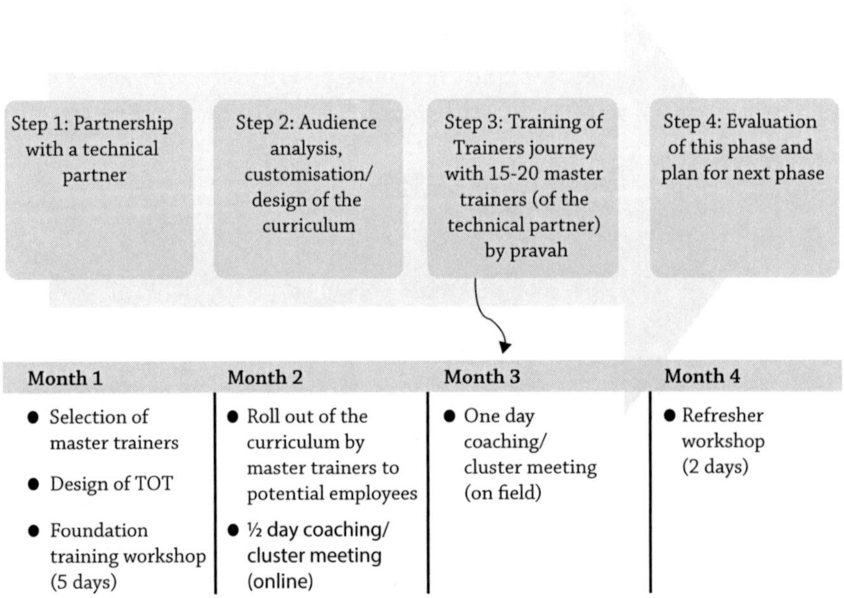

One such pilot currently being run is a project for technical upgradation of 2,500 two-wheeler roadside mechanics supported by Castrol India. The life competencies curriculum is 40 per cent of the total intervention. We have received very positive feedback from both the trainers and the mechanics. To our surprise, the life competency curriculum is actually serving as the pull for the mechanics as they realise that they are now able to reflect and articulate their aspirations, invest in building customer relations, manage their time better and apply the learning for effective decision-making. This, they all feel, will lead to an increase in their business. Six months remain of the project; we hope to draw much more learning from it.

Annex 5

Curriculum Framework

Broad Themes	*Objective of Sessions and Brief Description*	*Pedagogy*
Setting the context	• Building the need for change. • Co-creating/developing broad contours of the change with the group.	• Case study • Questionnaire
	Ability to Understand Self	
Aspiration building	Aspiration building is critical to young people entering the workforce. Learning to build aspirations for the trainers themselves, and helping youth participants in doing the same, down the line. Helping youth to build capacity to achieve their aspirations.	• Reflection • Case studies
Taking ownership	Ownership is critical to move from the space of blaming to claiming; to understand ones strengths and areas of improvement and move from a space of discontent to fulfilment and take leadership.	• Reflection • Games • Case studies
Ability to relate with empathy	Foregrounding empathy as a core value in building relationships with co-workers, bosses and subordinates. Understanding of ESCA and applying in personal and work life for improved relationships.	• Role play • Games
Ability to creating and interpret realities	Understand the role of stories to enhance critical thinking and analysis , ability to ask good questions to get to the bottom of the story.	• Role play • Games

Ability to learn	Establish learning as a critical life process and developing learner for life attitude. Exploring different learning styles of people, and understanding their own preferred style. Being open to learning, moving out of comfort zone, and learning through real world experiences.	• Demonstration • Reflection • Role plays
	Ability to Take Effective Decisions and Behaviours of Efficient, Effective, Happy and Desired Employees	
Efficient employee	The sessions will support the participants to develop the abilities such as goal setting, project management, decision-making, discipline and enhanced productivity to become an efficient employee.	• Reflection • Games • Case studies • Role play
Effective employee	The sessions will support the participants to develop the abilities such as customer orientation, empathy, health and well-being to become an effective employee.	• Reflection • Games • Case studies • Role play
Happy employee	The sessions will support the participants to develop the abilities such as positive relationships, handing cultural transitions, resolve conflicts, team work, financial literacy to become a happy employee.	• Reflection • Games • Case studies • Role play
Desired employee	The sessions will support the participants to develop the abilities such as wholesome leadership skills, congruency between inside and outside to become a desired employee.	• Reflection • Games • Case studies • Role play
	Ability to Align to Social Realities such as Religion, Caste, Gender, Class	
Social narratives Gender Cultural transition		

6

SANJAY SHARMA

Drug Menace in Punjab

Genesis, Scale and Control Measures

Scenario of Mounting Frustrations

This paper attempts to understand the nature and scale of the drug menace in Punjab and suggest measures to combat it. The State has earned a bad name as its young generation is harmed by easy availability of contraband drugs. Societal acceptance of intoxicants on the one hand and the frustration generated due to the decline of Punjab as an economic powerhouse on the other has aggravated the problem. Agriculture, the largest employer and money-churner in the state, is facing a crisis. Unemployment among the youth is rising. There is a marked downtrend in education and health facilities. Even in sports, Punjab has experienced a fall. The youth do not have meaningful, productive and continuous engagements to uphold their self-esteem. Limited employment opportunities have forced many farmers to sell off their small landholdings in order to send their children abroad in search of jobs. They are even migrating illegally. Thus, aspirations of the Punjabi youth are now linked to their prospects abroad, in the United States, Canada or Europe.

Under these circumstances, frustration is bound to envelop the young people. The Punjabis are more likely to be vulnerable to lows than other Indians, since a lavish lifestyle is part of their culture. They would proclaim *chand di kala* (literally, the ascending moon, meaning enjoy life) despite facing serious difficulties in their economic or personal lives.

The Punjab drug problem is thus related to its social and cultural features. A closer look at Goa and Kerala, other states which are also facing severe drug problem, shows that addiction in those states is caused by different reasons. For example, the spread of drug addiction in Goa can be attributed to the influence of foreign tourists.

Examining specific economic and social aspects would provide clues to the problem of drugs in Punjab. Incomes as well as aspirations rose during the Green Revolution, but within 20 years, the productivity and surpluses reached a plateau. The post-Green Revolution period started a crisis of identity in Punjab. It was followed by a two decade-long phase of terrorism. Punjab started to fall off the list of economically developing states. Even as the glory of the Green Revolution withered, those who had benefitted from it started trying drugs to get a kick. Field observations show that large numbers from the rural Sikh farming community took to drugs and intoxicants. In the militancy days, a host of people migrated to the United Kingdom, the United States, Canada and other developed countries. Remittances of migrants created a class with money to spend on a lavish lifestyle. Punjab thus developed a solid market for drugs.

Some Other Aggravating Factors

Employment: Bleak prospects for gainful employment is one of the principal causes of high drug use. The population of the State is 28 million. The population of youth (between 15 and 34), who can be termed as job-seekers, is estimated to be 18 million. Those studying and those working (including the underemployed) are 4.5 million each; the rest, about 9 million, are jobless. They are more vulnerable to addiction.

Education: The quality of education is deteriorating. A survey conducted by the Punjab Farmers Commission revealed that 5 per cent of the children of the 8th standard could not read books of the second standard. Nearly 70 per cent of those in the 3rd standard could not read a whole sentence. Only 62 per cent of the 8th standard students could divide and multiply.

There is also a serious dearth of professional training institutions. The share of public institutions among them is declining and the proportion of high-fee charging private institutions is rising. There are 250 private colleges and only 50 government ones. Similarly, while the private sector has 187 B.Ed colleges, the government has only 4. As against 10 government institutions dealing with health education (3 medical, 2 dental, 1 ayurvedic and 4 nursing colleges), there are 131 private bodies (7, 11, 11 and 102 respectively). The fee for an MBBS candidate selected through government mechanism in private medical college is ₹13.5 lakh, but the management quota seat goes for ₹41 lakh. The same education in a government medical college costs less than ₹5 lakh. The youth left out of this race for whatever reason are frustrated and vulnerable, especially since drugs are easily available and the culture tolerates the use of intoxicants.

Health: The health infrastructure has not grown after the 1980s. The State requires 4,500 health sub-centres as against the present 2,885, a number that has not changed since 1980. It still makes do with 1,192 dispensaries, the same number it had in 1980. It has also not been able to meet the minimum requirement of 700 health centres, the number of existing health centres being 426. The requirement of community health centres is 170, but their number is just 114. As against 82 sub-divisional hospitals needed in the state, the current availability is just 44. No rural health centre has emergency services. The minimum requirement of 4 specialists in a community health centre has not been met in any of the 114 health centres.

Health services are important as the first bulwark against drug addiction. The State has opened 40 de-addiction centres as parts of health centres, including an exclusive one for women in Ludhiana. Costly de-addiction and rehabilitation treatment also pushes sizeable numbers into abject economic conditions. Various cancers are spreading rapidly due to excessive use chemical fertilisers and pesticides.

Agriculture: Over the past few decades, worsening agriculture distress coupled with non-availability of industrial jobs has led to frustration among the rural youth. Fragmentation of landholdings and a break-down of the joint family system has taken away the cushion that softened the ups and downs of life.

Agriculture employs 35 per cent of the population. Its share in the state GDP (gross domestic product) is less than 17 per cent. Too many people thus share too meagre an income. The number of rural landowning households is coming down; it was about 14 lakh (64 per cent of the total) in 1971 and 11 lakh (20 per cent) in 2011.

A very large proportion of the rural households, 98 per cent, are in debt. A Centre for Research in Rural and Industrial Development study found farm debts to have increased 22 times during the last decade. In the six weeks between 1 April and 13 May 2016, 72 farmers committed suicide, possibly due to their indebtedness.

According to a Commission of Agriculture Cost and Prices report, the annual net returns from wheat and rice in Punjab average ₹36,000 per hectare or a monthly net income of just ₹3,000 per hectare, which is less than what domestic help in urban areas is generally paid. A decade-old National Sample Survey found that given a choice, 42 per cent of the farmers would like to quit their occupation.

Scale of Drug Menace

A United Nations report[1] says that Punjab is the second worst among the drug-affected Indian states. The extent and severity of substance addiction in Punjab as compared to the country is shown in Table 6.1.

Table 6.1

Substance Abuse: Punjab vis-ā-vis India

Substance	*Addicted Population, % of Total*	
	India	*Punjab*
Opium	1.0	3.4
Tobacco	26.0	58.0
Liquor	49.8	64.6

Source: http://www.unodc.org/doc/wdr2016/WORLD_DRUG_REPORT_2016_web.pdf

Though the religion of the majority community in the state, Sikhism, has sanctions against drugs and tobacco, their consumption is widespread. There are drug users in schools as well as in colleges. Thirty per cent of the girls surveyed said that they had tasted one

1. *World Drug Report, 2016 (http://www.unodc.org/doc/wdr2016/WORLD_DRUG_REPORT_2016_web.pdf))*

intoxicant or the other at least once. Punjab has had a long history of father and son consuming liquor together. Now a kind of new culture is developing where young siblings, brothers and sisters, are reportedly using narcotics together. As the male market for liquor is saturated, companies are earmarking funds to reach out to women.

Recently, the Punjab police announced that it would conduct dope tests on candidates for recruitment. Almost a fourth of the 6 lakh applicants did not turn up to be tested possibly because they were users. Incidentally, only 1 per cent of those tested were positive.

Newspaper reports suggested a four-fold increase in visits to de-addiction centres during the 2012 assembly elections. The police, under instructions from the Election Commission, cracked down on peddlers and addicts. As a result, addicts had to seek the help of doctors to cope with their withdrawal symptoms.

Some reports allege that migrant labour is offered poppy husk to enhance their capacity to work for long hours. The migrants are tempted to work longer to earn more money to send home, and drugs temporarily overcome their less than required nutrition intake through food.

Social and political impact: The negative impact of drug use is telling on the society. Chain-snatching has become a common crime and is on the rise due to drug addiction. There have been reports of sons killing their parents because the elders refused them money to get intoxicated. Addiction-affected families have had to sell their land. Marriages are breaking up and matrimonial alliances are becoming difficult to fix, as parents of marriageable girls do not trust the boys they meet.

It is said that a political party with penetration among drug-dependent voters can win elections just by supplying them drugs. Political experts say a party with access to criminals in villages is best placed to influence such voters. If a survey by the All-India Institute of Medical Sciences is to be believed, each of the 117 assembly constituencies has some 2,000 hard core drug addicts. Margins of victory between the two main parties, the Congress and the Akali Dal, have been very close during the last three elections. A swing of just a couple of per cent permits the winner to edge past the rival party. It seems thus that habitual drug addicts could possibly influence the outcome in at least a score of seats in such tightly-contested elections. That number could be much higher in the Malwa belt bordering the opium producing state of Rajasthan, which elects half the members of the Punjab assembly. A survey conducted in the 2000 found that more than 60 per cent of the households in the region consumed some intoxicant at one point of time.

Supply chains: The late Pakistani military dictator General Zia-ul-Haq aspired to become the leader of the Islamic world by fighting Russia in Afghanistan and "bleeding India through 100 cuts". He developed a network of informers in Afghanistan comprising opium growers. That network was engaged in exporting their produce. The best possible route was through Punjab. Terrorism in the 1990s gave smugglers an opportunity to push the contraband through Punjab in turmoil.

Punjab is in a particularly precarious position as it is surrounded by states and nations growing contraband—Rajasthan for opium, Himachal Pradesh for hashish and cannabis, and now Jammu and Kashmir and Pakistan, the main suppliers of the Afghan opium. The nearby Uttar Pradesh and Madhya Pradesh allow opium growing under license in certain areas. The latest development is contraband coming to Punjab from Myanmar via Delhi to fill the gap created by a tighter vigil on the India-Pakistan border. According to a Narcotic Control Bureau (NCB) source, the Maoist-hit Jharkhand and Bengal now have opium growers. Myanmar and Cambodia have also started growing it. Manipur and Arunachal are emerging as new sources.

Afghanistan produces 90 per cent of the world heroine. The old opium cultivator lobby is now part of the American intelligence network. The Taliban tried to break the back of opium growers before Americans bombed them out post 9/11. The output came down to just 185 tonnes from a high of 6,000 tonnes. But now the Taliban levy tax on poppy cultivators, provide them seeds and guarantee them access to markets and transportation. Their activities are financed by drug cartels. The Afghan drug lords have their own armies.

Helmand province of Afghanistan and the bordering Pakistani provinces of Baluchistan and Khyber Pakhtunkhwa are the major processing centres. Around 40 per cent of the Afghan opium is handled by Pakistani smugglers, 30 per cent by Iranians and rest by the Central Asian drug lords. Pakistani smugglers are estimated to generate a contraband trade worth USD 2 billion a year. Last year, 300 kg of heroine was recovered by different agencies from the border. It is estimated that only 10 per cent of contraband is detected for various reasons, including corruption in the security agencies.

The Punjab border accounts for half the seizures of heroine in India. Therefore, Punjab has problems of both halting the supply from international and interstate routes and controlling the demand.

Addictive synthetic drugs are a new challenge, given the strong pharmaceutical base of the country, especially in the neighbourhood of Punjab at Baddi in Himachal Pradesh. These pharmaceutical units are now a potential threat, especially because of the shortage of drug inspectors. For example, 7,000 injections were recovered from a factory in Roorki. The police have also detected a few cases in which medicines were sent out under wrong labels. Investigations in several instances revealed that liquor addicts are now switching over to the cheaper synthetic drugs. Prescription records of users are not made available despite being mandatory.

Difficulties faced by official agencies: In India, NCB is not allowed to operate under-cover, unlike its counterpart in the United States. It does not have adequate staff or appropriate technology. The staff are so few that NCB dare not enter a place without the help of the Punjab police. With the spread of social media, the advantage of monitoring through phone-tapping has vanished. The use of women as couriers is increasing, since the number of policewomen is insufficient to intercept them. Many courier women are acquitted even after their arrest because the arresting police party is often unable to prove that a woman officer on the spot had frisked them.

On the other hand, the volume of trade and the profit margin are so huge that if a person is caught, the children and women folk in the same family continue with the job. A 10-year-old estimate showed that while the price of heroine at the source was ₹50,000 a kg, it was worth around ₹20 lakh per kg when it landed in Punjab, after due processing and the international quoted price was ₹5 crore per kg. Such huge margins attract innumerable risk takers who hope to grow rich through just one attempt of smuggling. Being lucky once is enough to make somebody a millionaire. This has tempted a large number of people to engage in this trade. A couple of years ago, 25,000 users and peddlers of contraband were in jail.

Smugglers know that drug supply can be safely ensured if a courier becomes an addict. Such a person would be left with no option but to sell drugs to earn money to feed the habit. This process creates an army of user-couriers.

Despite all its efforts, the government is seen as being so weak in dealing with the crisis that the Punjab and Haryana High Court is monitoring the policy formation with the help of an amicus curiae.

The Way Out

It is not easy to completely end drug use. There has not so far been a completely successful formula to eliminate drug use anywhere in the world. Yet the damage addiction causes requires a serious attempt to curtail and regulate drug abuse. This has to be seen in the larger perspective, as also the remedy. The problem is enormous. Therefore handling it in a casual or unscientific way is not going to help. The first requirement is that the State government should commission a survey to estimate correctly the incidence of drug use and addiction in different sections of the society, and put in place a procedure to periodically measure the problem in all its dimensions.

It should be recognised that the first prerequisite for deterring a young man or woman to be a drug user is his or her dignified, productive and regular engagement in the society, economy and polity. In turn, this requires that the citizens must be healthy, educated and enlightened. It is the responsibility of the state to ensure that every youth has access to affordable quality education and essential health services. The accelerated withdrawal of the state from education and health sectors after the 1990s in the liberalisation era has aggravated the drug menace is no coincidence.

It is believed that economic development and resultant prosperity brings in its wake large-scale drug addiction. As the country has embarked on a rapid development path, it is all the more necessary that measures are taken at this initial stage. The real action will be at the states' level. Every state need to be prepared to face the problem before it becomes unmanageable. Punjab now has an opportunity to show the way to other seriously affected states and territories, such as Goa, Manipur and the National Capital Region.

Promotion of sports could curb drug abuse. Punjab has scores of village clubs supported by local donors. They have shown good results. The government has also started promoting local clubs and health centres with very generous grants. However, availability of appropriate playgrounds is a major difficulty. Punjab, which once had a reputation of being a sports powerhouse, is now in the also-ran category, in contrast to the neighbouring state of Haryana. The education system must also recognise sports as a necessary tool of life training. Students should get credits for their achievements in sports.

Drug abuse and rehabilitation of the addicts should be treated as parts of the larger healthcare programme, with facilities to identify individuals at risk. Scientific evidence suggests that psychological tests can predict vulnerability to drugs at an early stage, and one out of six addicts can be readily cured. The government needs to create an infrastructure of medical centres attached to schools, colleges and youth activity centres to provide counselling and medical support.

Education needs an overhaul. Quality education at minimum cost needs to be within reach of each individual. Education needs to create employable youths who are culturally conscious, socially alert and progressive in their outlook. It should aim at promoting students' critical and creative faculties, and respect for their traditional values. Depiction of Punjabi culture as Bohemian in popular songs glorifying drinking should be discouraged. The people of Punjab traditionally value equality and justice. They make good entrepreneurs. They are less dogmatic and believe in hard work rather than in miracles. But today an impression is created that political, economic and social power is concentrated in a few hands, and intolerance and orthodoxy are rising. The youth should be encouraged to raise questions.

The government must engage institutions such as Dera Sacha Sauda, Radha Soami Satsang Beas and Divyajyoti Jagran Sansthan to rein in drug abuse. Gurdwaras and Shiromani Gurdwara Parbandhak Committee have to come together to fight the drug menace culturally, educationally, socially and economically.

One of the biggest challenges the government faces is that those sent to de-addiction centres are not welcomed back in society and remain unemployed. This makes them vulnerable to drug use again. The government should devise a strategy aimed at providing them opportunities for gainful employment and a respectable place in the society. This will make other drug addicts to follow their example.

Most of the measures suggested are related to reducing the demand for drugs, but there are supply side issues also. It is suspected that monitoring agencies turn a blind eye due to the involvement of big money. An increased presence of police and a proliferation of agencies have not been able to check the fast growth of drug use. The number of inspectors and their competence to identify camouflaged drugs as well as new technological devices used by drug smugglers should be enhanced.

A new approach involving the government and civil society needs to be tried out. Village or *mohalla* level anti-drug committees should be formed to keep the state machinery on its toes. These committees should be empowered to report drug availability, and, at the same time, take steps to rehabilitate the people who want to come out of drug addiction. They should be allowed to monitor local health and education facilities in order to check drug abuse.

As of now, the people affected by the drug menace do not have a say in fighting the problem. These committees should involve all stakeholders. They can create social awareness and isolate those who are involved in the drug trade. Such anti-social elements will be afraid to face committees comprising right-thinking local people.

7

S. MOHANAKUMAR

Demographic Transition and Employability of Youth in Kerala

Introduction

The decadal population growth rate in Kerala of 4.9 per cent is well below the national average of 17.1 per cent. The state has moved towards zero growth during 2001-2011, with two districts in the negative growth zone. This demographic transition in Kerala is characterised by a decline in the age group 0-14 and growing older age population. The working age population is growing but rather slowly. Another feature of the demographic transition is a relatively higher proportion of female job-seekers, caused by higher literacy rate and higher sex ratio (1,084 females per 1,000 males). The Kerala unemployment rate is higher as compared to the national average. In addition, the proportion of job-seekers with general as well as technical education has been growing rapidly, posing serious challenge of employability for professional education in the state.

This study reviews the demographic status of the Kerala economy from the perspective of unemployment and youth. It also evaluates critically the effectiveness of different programmes of the state and Central governments in skilling the job-seekers and youth of Kerala.

Demographics and Youth in Kerala

The definition of youth varies by country and time. A fluid definition to include those who have completed secondary or higher secondary education and are waiting for their first job appears to be appropriate to represent the youth in India. A more formal definition of youth comprising the age group 15-29, is adopted by the Youth Policy of India 2014.

The debate on demographic dividend is primarily centred around the question whether a young population is a blessing or a threat. The answer depends on how the country taps the productiveness of the youth through policies, schemes and programmes to actively engage them in the labour market. Youth, however, is a heterogeneous population entity possessing varied skills and demanding different avenues of employment. As they belong to and are nurtured in different social and economic milieus, their aspirations also differ. Therefore, it is rather difficult to think of homogeneous modes of intervention to meet the expectations of youth.

Kerala has the highest unemployment rate in the country, three times the national average. Youth in the 15-29 age group account for 23 per cent of the total population of the state. The unemployment rate for females among the youth is 47 per cent and 10 per cent for the males, 22 per cent in rural areas and 18 per cent in towns and cities. Daily unemployment status is higher than the weekly status, reflecting on intermittent unemployment.

Figure 7.1 shows unemployment rates of male and female youth in Kerala as compared to the same in India according to rural and urban areas.

Figure 7.1

Youth Unemployment Rate in Kerala and India, 2011-12

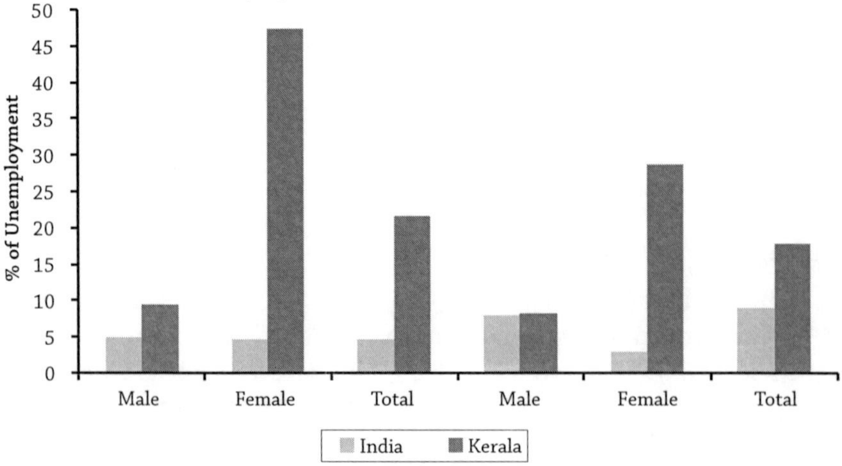

Source: National Sample Survey, January 2014.

To realise the demographic dividend, youth needs to be mainstreamed by being skilled and employed. The following questions assume special significance in this context: i) what type of skills does the productive sector of the economy require to absorb the unemployed youth? ii) what skills do the job-seekers possess? and iii) what should be the rate of growth for each sector to absorb the reserve labour force?

The number of job-seekers registered with employment exchanges and live in the employment registers can be taken as a crude index of the magnitude of the problem. Kerala had 3.6 million job-seekers in 2015, more than half of whom were females. Only 5 per cent of the job-seekers had technical and professional qualifications while 95 per cent had a general education background with little specific employable skills. ITI certificate holders (post 12th standard) and engineering diploma holders constituted more than 80 per cent of the job-seekers with technical and professional qualifications. Further, their numbers have been on the rise. Medical and engineering graduates accounted for 3 per cent and 14 per cent respectively of the professional category. Agricultural graduates were less than 1 per cent.

This observed trend shows a shortage of employable skills even among job-seekers with technical and professional training. This is known in literature as the two-box disease, which indicates a divorce between vocational training requirements and higher education, resulting in educated youth remaining non-employable.

Sustained job creation demands innovation, high value-addition and productivity growth. We need to examine the major sectors of the Kerala economy for their employment potential and prospects.

Kerala agriculture is dominated by plantation crops. Traditional farm folk have been abandoning their vocation in view of the crisis of crop production. Youth is dissuaded to take up agriculture because agriculture accounts for only 11 per cent of the net state domestic product but employs 20 per cent of the workforce. There is also a mismatch between crop production work availability and the composition of the unemployed youth. Agriculture does not use labour productively or efficiently and does not use the acquired skills effectively.

The secondary sector could be a potential avenue of absorbing a large mass of unemployed youth. However, manufacturing has a share of only 11 per cent in the gross state domestic product as compared to 18 per cent in the country. Service sector is a broad category encompassing several activities which require varied skills. The growing information technology sector does not require people with general qualifications. Further, skills in demand have been rapidly changing. Whether the prevailing higher education, especially technical education in ITIs, needs overhauling and if so, in which direction and in what mode are the questions that emerge in this context.

Table 7.1

Qualification-wise Registrations with Kerala Employment Exchanges

Year	*% Registrations with Qualification*				
	Below SSLC	*SSLC*	*Higher Secondary*	*Graduation*	*Post-Graduation*
2005	17.1	59.4	15.7	6.3	1.5
2006	16.5	60.0	16.0	6.0	1.4
2007	15.8	60.7	16.2	6.0	1.3
2008	15.0	61.5	16.5	5.7	1.3
2009	14.5	62.2	16.5	5.6	1.2
2010	13.8	62.4	16.7	6.1	1.1
2011	13.5	62.8	16.6	6.0	1.1
2012	13.3	63.1	16.7	5.9	1.1
2013	11.7	63.2	17.5	6.2	1.6
2014	10.5	63.1	18.4	6.6	1.4
2015	11.6	62.2	19.4	6.5	0.3
Average annual growth, %	-1.0	2.3	3.7	1.9	-10.9

Source: *Economic Review 2015*, Government of Kerala.

In view of the current Kerala situation, these issues need to be examined in the context of the large immigration of unskilled and semi-skilled youth from other states, particularly West Bengal, Assam and Bihar. Reasons for their immigration and the type of jobs they perform would then have to be contrasted with what type of jobs the migrant labour from Kerala to West Asia hold and their skills.

In light of the above, the Kerala youth appear to be suffering from a multiple-box-disease rather than the two-box disease. These multiple boxes, if not resolved, could be potential threats to the democratic fabric of the country, instead of the demographic dividend being a blessing.

Table 7.1 shows the distribution of job-seekers registered with Kerala employment exchanges from 2005 to 2015.

The points to note are that the numbers of non-SSLC (secondary school leaving certificate) and more substantially, post-graduate job-seekers, have declined during the last decade while those of the others have increased.

Trend in Job-seekers with Professional and Technical Qualifications

Job-seekers can be classified into two groups, those with general education or without any specialised skills and professionally and technically qualified ones. It is common knowledge that the former have relatively fewer market opportunities than the latter. Since the cost of professional education exceeds that of general education, the cost of being unemployed is higher for the latter segment. Some 53 per cent of the 1.62 lakh professional job-seekers in 2015 had ITI diplomas. Another 28 per cent had engineering diplomas and 15 per cent were engineering graduates. The number of unemployed engineering graduates has increased from 6,000 to 25,000 during the last decade. Medical graduates constituted 2 per cent and agriculture and veterinary graduates 1 per cent (Table 7.2). The high proportion of ITI diploma holders is because the market for them employs engineering graduates for the same remuneration. There are no private institutions in the agricultural sector. This explains the low proportion of agricultural graduates. Figure 7.2 shows the rate of growth of professional job-seekers during 2005-2015.

Table 7.2

Shares of Unemployed Technical/Professionals in Kerala, 2005-2015

Year	*% Share in Unemployment of Persons with Qualifications in Kerala*					
	Medicine	*Engineering*	*Engineering (Diploma)*	*ITI*	*Agriculture*	*Veterinary*
2005	1.9	3.6	23.4	70.3	0.5	0.3
2006	1.8	5.2	25.4	66.9	0.5	0.3
2007	1.6	5.1	23.6	68.9	0.5	0.4
2008	1.6	5.5	22.2	69.9	0.5	0.4
2009	1.7	6.5	24.8	66.2	0.4	0.4
2010	1.4	5.4	23.4	69.3	0.3	0.3
2011	1.5	6.7	23.0	68.2	0.3	0.3
2012	1.7	8.5	22.9	66.2	0.3	0.4
2013	1.8	23.9	22.7	51.0	0.3	0.4
2014	2.2	16.3	25.5	55.1	0.5	0.5
2015	2.2	14.7	28.3	53.9	0.6	0.3

Source: Estimated from *Economic Review 2015*, Government of Kerala.

Figure 7.2

Rate of Growth of Professional Job-seekers 2005-2015

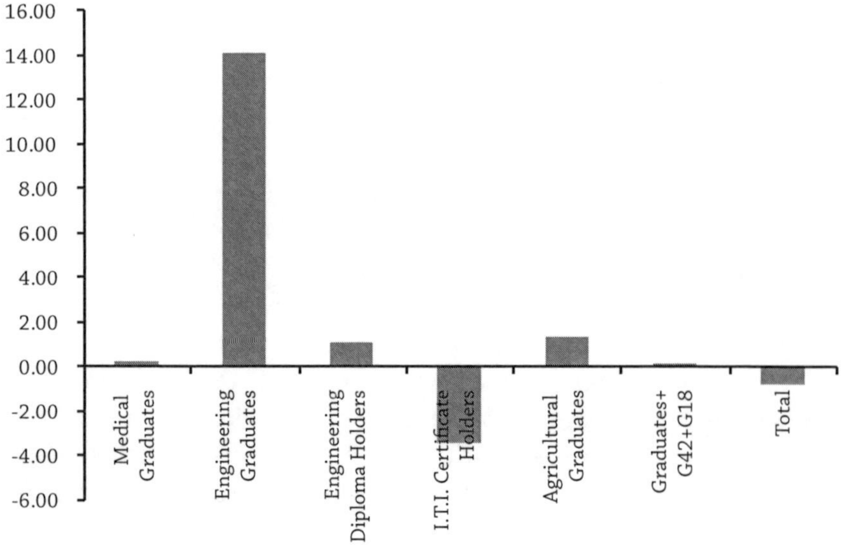

Source: Computed from Table 7.2.

The National Skill Development Mission envisages Kerala to train 1.5 lakh to 2 lakh persons annually to reach the national target of 500 million-strong skilled manpower by 2022. The state higher education department has launched an ASAP (additional skill acquisition programme) for the unemployed youth. It intends to impart industry-specific skills along with sector-specific skills such as English communication. Its spread and acceptance have been poor because it fails to prepare the youth for the prestigious jobs they aspire for.

The government often floats the argument that since the graduates could migrate to other states and countries for jobs leading to an outflow of resources from Kerala, the responsibility of the government is limited to providing them with the opportunity to get education at a low cost. The higher educational department decided to permit private initiative without taking into account emerging needs of the job market. That has resulted in youths in massive numbers unable to find placement either within the state or outside. There is also a substantial decline in the number of ITI diploma-holders, from 1.25 lakh to 80,000 from 2005 to 2015, as the diploma-holders realised that their education and acquired skills have little relevance in the labour market. This is a huge waste of not only trained manpower, but also of precious household resources expended on education.

Neither professional education institutions nor skill development/ vocational training centres have succeeded in their avowed objective. ITIs and nursing colleges were the preferred slots for private capital when professional education sector in the state was opened up during the late 1990s and the early 2000s. The unemployment situation of ITI diploma holders and nurses points to a policy fatigue in the education sector in the state and a mismatch between the talents possessed by the workforce and the skills required by the industry.

Skill Upgradation Plans and Schemes in Kerala

Several programmes and schemes for upgradation of skills exist in Kerala. It was the first state in India to announce as early as 1982 unemployment allowance to those who have registered in employment exchanges. Under the scheme, unemployed youths with SSLC pass registered and live on the register for three years consecutively are eligible for an unemployment assistance of ₹120 per month, if their family income is below ₹12,000 a year and personal income below ₹100 per month. Since 1988, local self-governments in their respective areas have disbursed the amount to unemployed youth.

The additional skill acquisition programme of the higher education department is one of the major schemes for skilling up the youth for placement in job markets. Initiated in 2012-13, it aims at enhancing the avenues of employability of students passing out of higher secondary schools and colleges. In addition to their regular curriculum, students are imparted skills required by the industry. The State government has widened the scheme with the support of Asian Development Bank from 2014. Yet there are very few takers as the scheme does not enable the students to be placed in prestigious jobs of their choice. Many students, particularly girls, do not opt for it because it is conducted in the evenings.

Other important schemes in Kerala for upgrading skills and placement possibilities of educated youth are presented in Table 7.3. Many of these have been thought of by the government very recently, especially during the last five years. Schemes and programmes have been introduced and managed without adequate evaluation of the past and therefore, schemes in the old format with unchanged age-old syllabi and curriculum are more or less replicated and announced in every budget. As a result, they fail to attract youth.

These programmes have not addressed the challenges of employability of youths in Kerala as identified by the Expert Committee of the State Planning Board in the 12th Five-Year Plan period. They include limited industry participation, absence of industry-readiness among the vocationally trained students, and a limited awareness or uptake of skill development initiatives among the youth. There has been little attempt to find long-lasting solutions to these challenges.

Table 7.3

Schemes and Programmes for Youth Skill Upgradation/Placement in Kerala

Scheme		*Objective*	*Targets Fulfilled*
Comprehensive Mission on Employment Generation (MEGA)		To provide holistic direction to self employment programmes, implemented by government agencies.	Recently initiated.
Kerala State Self-Development Mission	1.	To inculcate entrepreneurial confidence among youth.	Launch 2,000 ventures every year.
	2.	To provide interest-free loans up to ₹2 million.	Provide employment to 20,000 persons annually.
Employability Centre	1.	To convert employment exchanges into employability centres.	6 per cent of the total registrants in employment exchanges were covered under the scheme.
	2.	To identify skill gap of registrants.	
	3.	To provide skill gap training for placement.	
Mission on employment generation		To provide direction to self-employment programme.	
Job portal under Department of Training		To facilitate employment opportunities to skilled workers and professionals.	20,000 trainees pass out every year. Job portal is accessed by employers worldwide.
Kerala Academy for Skills Excellence		To facilitate mass human resource development through specialised skill development courses.	A government company has been formed in Kollam district to undertake training.

Source: Compiled from *Economic Review*, Government of Kerala, relevant years.

Conclusion

There is a serious disconnect between education and employability of youth in Kerala. Programmes to upgrade skills of the educated youth to enable them to be employed are not found to be effective and therefore, there is a double-box disease as characterised in the literature. This situation is not significantly different from that in other states, which is symptomatic of the shortcomings of manpower planning in India. The disconnect exists because the education system with its syllabi and curriculum has not been subjected to overhauling in view of the dynamic inputs. Professional learning has to be updated and thoroughly integrated with the workplace. This is hugely lacking in our system. The unregulated entry and dominance of private capital in the professional and technical education sectors have further aggravated the crisis. Students are attracted by the title of the course or degree rather than its content and relevance to employability. The massive production of degree-holders leads to a supply in excess of demand. This causes a segment of the labour force to be underpaid in comparison to their counterparts elsewhere. The underpayment or non-remunerative employment degrades the labour force in terms of their physical and cultural abilities. The State has to ensure that labour is gainfully engaged.

8

KANCHAN MATHUR

Exploring Education, Employment and Citizenship

A Case Study of Youth in Rajasthan

Social Context of Rajasthan

With an area of 342,000 sq km (10.4 per cent of India), Rajasthan, located in the north-west of the country, is India's largest state. It has a population of 69 million (6 per cent of India, and the eight largest in the country). The state is divided into 33 districts, with 297 towns and over 44,000 villages. The share of youth[1] in the population is 34 per cent in rural areas and 37 per cent in urban areas (35 per cent overall). The rural youth population is 2.7 times higher than the urban youth. Hence, any policy and programme for youth in the state must focus on the diversity, capacity and needs of this segment of the population.

Census 2011 shows the share of the youth among the SCs (scheduled castes) to be higher than that among the STs (scheduled tribes). Around 18 per cent of the state's youth was from SC communities, while 13 per cent belonged to ST. The share of females in youth population was lower than that of the males in all categories: total, rural, urban and SC/ST.

Rajasthan is primarily an agrarian economy. The total cultivated area is about 20 million ha, of which only 20 per cent is irrigated. Nearly two-thirds of the total area of the state is arid or semi-arid with low and irregular rainfall, characterised by extremes of climate. The Indira Gandhi Canal irrigates north-western Rajasthan, canals from Haryana and Uttar Pradesh serve the north and the Narmada

1. Youth generally refers to people in the age group of 15 to 34 years.

provides water to the south. Ground water is available at an average depth of over 60 m. Irregular and uncertain rainfall and frequent droughts cause various risks, uncertainties and stress situations to households with fragile livelihood bases, directly impacting their access to resources.

The state and especially several western districts experience recurrent droughts which create a catastrophic situation. While the severity of the drought may be of a short duration, its impact on people's livelihood and survival strategies could be persistently adverse, such as loss of land, livestock, household goods and valuables. Debt and bondage could be the natural results. Under-employment or work at extremely low wages and migration to cities, both within the state and outside, could be widespread.

Water availability is a core issue in many parts of the state. Ground water has been exploited all over the state to unsustainably high levels. The average exploitation of ground water as a percentage of annual recharge is 125, which means that for every litre that percolates into the ground, 1.25 litres are taken out. Over the long run, this would increase the desertification of the state, as also make ground water more brackish and mineralised on account of concentration of salts and render soils poorer. A further issue is the predominance of small ruminants in the cattle population. The sheep damage vegetative cover because of their browsing habits, which could upset the balance between fodder and cattle. Pasture management is a critical issue, not just for development, but also for environmental safety.

Material power, an ownership of property and assets, is traditionally vested in men in Rajasthan. Though women's contribution to agricultural production is well recognised, a considerable gender disparity exists. Women continue to lack land ownership rights, despite the fact that majority of them work as agricultural wage-labourers or on farms owned by members of their families. This lack of resource endowment coupled with low social and human capital among women leads to their further marginalisation.

Rajasthan is characterised by a feudal history, stringent patriarchy, rigid gender norms and deep-rooted disadvantages which pervade all spheres of domestic and social life. Women's identity and roles continue to be defined through their (subordinated) relationship to men. The 2011 Census figures also show an alarming drop in the sex ratio in the 0-6 age group from 909 in 2001 to 883 in 2011. This decline of 26 points indicates a clear bias against the girl-child. A male-child is the preferred choice, resulting in discrimination against the girl-child right from the time she is born, reflected in the distribution of food, nutrition, healthcare; education or freedom; rights and justice. This cycle of disadvantages begins at birth and continues throughout her life.

One of the most crucial indicators of status of women in any society is the sex ratio. Census 2011 shows that the overall sex ratio has improved from 921 to 926 over the last decade. This is the highest recorded for the state since 1901, but it is still below the national average of 940. While the state has made some improvement in human development indicators in the last decade, it still faces the challenge of achieving gender equality in access to health, nutrition and education.

The Rajasthan maternal mortality ratio (MMR) continues to be amongst the highest in the country. Incidence of malnutrition is also high despite great improvements in food production and distribution. The percentage of anaemia among women in general is rising, as it is among women in the childbearing age as well.

The educational profile of Rajasthan has been changing, albeit at a slow pace. The overall literacy rate grew from 60 per cent in 2001 to 67 per cent in 2011. The gender gap between male and female literacy rates is huge, with 80 and 53 per cent respectively. Seventeen districts show female literacy rates of under 50 per cent.

Field evidence shows girls constituting the major group in government schools across caste groups, but enrolment of Muslim girls continues to be low. While the gender gap in primary education is closing, that in upper primary and secondary levels continues to be a challenge. Ensuring regular participation of girls in the schooling system, however, is constrained by various socio-cultural norms and attitudes as well as gender roles and responsibilities, early marriage and gender biases. This impacts adversely the employment and livelihood security opportunities for young women.

Women work primarily in agriculture where their proportion is significantly higher than that of men. They perform all the back-breaking chores. They are disempowered, low-skilled, and in many cases, represent the residual labour force. They have fewer occupational choices owing to poor geographic mobility and education or skills. Their wages are lower in comparison to the men for equal amount and duration of work. The out-migration of men leaves women particularly vulnerable as they have to bear the additional burden of securing livelihoods in these situations; however, women's roles are regarded as neither productive nor work. The status of girls/ women, closely intertwined with the harsh environmental conditions causing excessive work burden on them, suffers badly. This is a major problem in the social context of the state that is extremely orthodox with rigid and rather unequally-defined caste and gender relations.

Situation of Youth in Rajasthan

Literacy Status

Literacy plays a vital role in capacitating the labour force. Not only the probability of being skilled is higher among the literate youth, but it also enables them to read better the labour market parameters and take relevant decisions, such as whether to work at a particular wage rate, the preferred nature of work and the other terms and conditions of employment. Nearly 75 per cent of the Rajasthan youth is literate (males 88 per cent, females 61 per cent). The gender gap is higher among rural youth at 32 per cent[2] as against 12 per cent in urban areas.[3]

Employment/Work Profile

The state is experiencing an ever widening gap between the demand and supply of labour. The mismatch is reflected in both unavailability of work at a given wage and unavailability of desired work. It is estimated that out of the total youth population, 40 per cent are main workers, 19 per cent marginal workers, and non-

2. Males: 86 per cent and female:54 per cent in rural areas.

3. Males: 91 per cent and females:79 per cent in urban areas.

workers constitute 40 per cent. The high number of work-seekers[4] in the state clearly underscores the mismatch between the types of work available, wages offered and types of demand made by the available workforce. In both rural and urban areas, the share of females among marginal workers and non-workers is noticeably higher than their male counterparts. Around 51 per cent of the young work-seekers are male and 49 per cent female. The share of females among non-workers is higher in both rural (56 per cent) and urban (67 per cent) areas. The share of females among work-seekers is higher in rural (49 per cent) compared to urban areas (46 per cent). It is important to flag that three in every five marginal or non-workers are females.

Work-seekers by Literacy Status

Of the total youth work-seekers, 28 per cent are illiterate irrespective of the place of residence. Illiteracy among females work-seekers is much higher at 44 per cent as compared to only 12 per cent among men. Three in every four non-literate work-seekers are women. Rural women have a 79 per cent share in the non-literate urban work-seekers as against 65 per cent in rural areas.

Work Classification by Educational Level

Almost half (48 per cent in all, 53 per cent in rural areas, 31 per cent in urban) of the nearly 3 million literate work-seekers have not completed secondary school education. Marginally more males (32 per cent) belong to this group compared to females (31 per cent). In urban Rajasthan, 35 per cent of literate female work-seekers are graduates; the corresponding figure among men is 26 per cent.

Literacy and Employability

Rajasthan has 22 universities, 1,610 colleges, 64 engineering colleges, 71 polytechnics and industrial training institutes and 75 MBA institutes (ICRA 2015).[5] It has approximately 50,000 primary and 39,000 middle/secondary schools. The gross enrolment ratio

4. Work-seekers are those marginal and non-workers, who are available for/seeking work. In the state, 39,05,525 youth are work-seekers i.e., 28 per cent of total marginal and non-workers.

5. *Mapping of Human Resources and Skills for Rajasthan—2015* (Executive Summary), Government of Rajasthan, Executive Summary, and ICRA Management Consulting Services Limited.

in 2010 among 14-15 year olds was 62 per cent. The gender parity index in 2010 ranged from 0.93 at the elementary level to 0.69 at the secondary level, both lower than the national average.

Rajasthan has a high school dropout rate, being 50 per cent from the primary to the upper primary levels. The pass percentage is low (50 per cent in SSC and 68 per cent in HSC examinations). The educational attainment levels among youth are considerably lower in the state than in India overall, and gender differences in enrolment and attainment substantially wider.

The state has fewer employment opportunities for youth. Unemployment rates are slightly higher among young people than among the general population (64 per cent young men were employed during the last 12 months as against 48 per cent young women). Currently, there are over 7.5 lakh unemployed persons in the state. Around 24 per cent of the engineering degree-holders and 26 per cent diploma-holders are unemployed. Graduates of the arts and science colleges are not geared for jobs in the industry since these courses are not employment-oriented.

The unemployability of the Rajasthan students graduating from its formal education system highlights the poor quality of education on offer due to:

i. Disconnect between academic curricula and industry requirements, resulting in deficiencies in specific functional skills, besides lack of practical training, market-orientation, and soft skills;
ii. Shortage of appropriately trained faculty, which is a concern of increasing significance.

These issues, if left unaddressed, will widen the skill gaps that Rajasthan needs to close to realise its economic growth objectives. The new employment opportunities not only call for enhanced functional skills, but also sector-specific competencies at all levels and several soft skills.

Substance Abuse

The quality of education being out of sync with the demands of the job market impacts the self-esteem of the youth. Drugs become the first crutch of support for the alienated youngsters. A recent article reports that Rajasthan might be competing with the neighbouring Punjab in the menace of drug addiction. Some 20 per cent of the population is reportedly addicted to opium, of whom 80 per cent are literate. Another study shows that 25 per cent of the children in Rajasthan are addicted to injectable drugs. In many villages, unqualified, self-styled doctors give medical advice and provide medicines, including sedatives, to youth.

Marital Status

Rajasthan has the highest percentage in the country (32 per cent) of girls being married before the legal age of 18 years. Child marriages contribute to maintaining the intergenerational cycles of poverty, leading to further marginalisation of women in the society. Many factors, such as poverty, a perception that marriage will provide protection, family honour, social norms, customary or religious laws that condone the practice, an inadequate legislative framework and the state of the country's civil registration system, contribute to the prevalence of child marriages. They often compromise a girl's development by early pregnancies and social isolation, interrupting schooling, limiting opportunities for career and vocational advancement and increasing the risk of domestic violence.[6]

Health Profile

The sexual and reproductive health profile of Rajasthan youth highlights its vulnerability. Marriage continues to take place before the legal minimum age for both young women and men. The median age at first marriage in the state is 16.3 years (Annual Health Survey 2011-12) and that at child birth is 19.6 years (NFHS III).[7] While sexual relations are initiated early and within the marriage for large proportions of young men and women in Rajasthan, sexual risk-taking before marriage is not unknown: 9 per cent and 2 per cent of

---

6. *http://data.unicef.org/child-protection/child-marriage.html#sthash.TvJcsmBi.dpuf*

7. *Annual Health Survey 2011-12*, Fact Sheet Rajasthan, Vital Statistics Division, Office of the Registrar General & Census Commissioner, India, New Delhi, website: *www.censusindia.gov.in*

unmarried young men and women respectively, aged 15 between 24 years, had engaged in sexual relations (IIPS and Population Council 2009).[8]

Despite this early initiation of sexual relations, available evidence suggests that young people's knowledge of sexual and reproductive health tends to be limited. Some 46 per cent of male youth have comprehensive knowledge of HIV as compared to 38 per cent of the women. Similarly, sexual and reproductive healthcare seeking is limited: two-fifths and almost three-fifths of the married and the unmarried young men and women respectively reported that they would be uncomfortable about approaching a healthcare provider for contraceptives. Maternal care-seeking among married adolescent girls in rural areas of the state was far more limited than that experienced by adult women.

More women (84 per cent) than men (78 per cent) in the age group 15-24 are aware of the pill as a spacing method. In the same age group, a higher percentage of men (92 per cent) are aware of the use of the condom than women (73 per cent). Around 45 per cent women and 83 per cent men had heard of HIV/AIDS. A fifth of the youth were aware of contraceptive practices.

Increasing Violence Against Women

National Crimes Research Bureau (NCRB) data for the last 20 years shows that the incidence of crime against women in Rajasthan is higher than that in the country (Figure 8.1). This raises serious concerns about safety and security of young women in the state.

The NCRB data also demonstrate that most of the violence against women takes place at the domestic level (Figure 8.2). The violence/crime against women was the highest in 2015. Major crimes against women are rape, kidnapping and assault on women with the intent to outrage her modesty.

Besides these reported crimes, women also face myriad forms of violence. The widespread preference for sons and aversion to

8. IIPS and Population Council Youth in India (2007). *Situation & Needs, 2006-2007*, website: *http://www.iipsindia.org or http://iipsindia.org/pdf/India%20Report.pdf*

daughters is the most obvious manifestation of gender discrimination. The tradition of female infanticide in several communities of Rajasthan has been well-documented. Ready and easy availability of sex determination techniques is leading to widespread sex-selective abortions. The sex ratio is adverse at all stages of women's lives. While the adult sex ratio has shown a slight improvement in favour of women, the child sex ratio in the 0-6 age group continues to show a decline.

Figure 8.1

Crimes against Women in Rajasthan

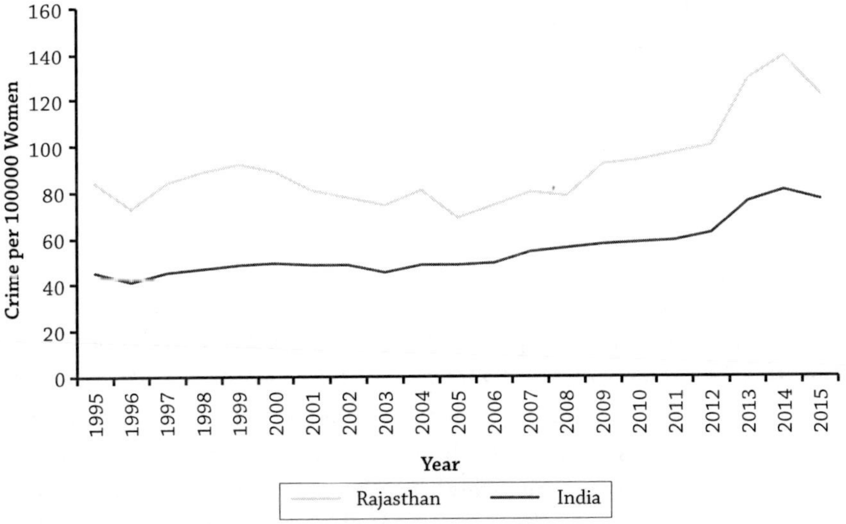

Source: National Crime Records Bureau, Government of India, 2015.

This increasing number of missing girls and women leads to serious concerns about the strains on the social and moral fabric of communities and regions. Field observations confirm an increase in sexual violence against women, buying of brides who are often abducted and trafficked, conditional marriages, and distorted customs of cohabitation and marriage such as age-mismatched marriages, polyandry, and coercive sex by multiple male family members. Labelling of women as witches and being forced to go into nata are other forms of violence inflicted on them.

Figure 8.2

Trend of Major Crimes in Rajasthan

Source: National Crime Records Bureau, Government of India.

The stronghold of *jati* panchayats and *khaaps* in rural areas forces families into performing their prescribed responsibility towards girls, including controlling their sexual behaviour to protect family honour. After their marriage, the girls' education and opportunities for socio-economic empowerment are severely restricted. *Khaap* and religious leaders also pronounce regressive judgements that violate women's right of choice and agency. Innate conservatism and diktats of community leaders have led to reported cases of honour crimes in many instances.

Skill Development Schemes to Empower Youth

Several Rajasthan line departments have launched skill development schemes to empower the workforce engaged in different sectors. Rajasthan was one of the first states in the country to set up a skills mission, the Rajasthan Skill and Livelihood Mission Rajasthan (RMoL) in 2004. It is the apex policy body for skill development.

RMoL has now been restructured on the pattern of the skills mission of the Government of India. It comprises the Rajasthan Council for Skill and Livelihood Development, a policymaking body headed by the Chief Minister and Rajasthan Skills and Livelihood Development Corporation to scale-up skill training programmes. Several other agencies for skill upgradation have been set up under its aegis, including the Rajasthan Knowledge Corporation, Rajasthan Council of Vocational Education and Training and Rajasthan Skill Development Initiative Society. It has recently established new institutions such as Rajasthan Institute of Security Education and construction academies. It is making an effort to generate employment opportunities in sectors such as construction, textiles, healthcare, tourism, hospitality, food processing, gems and jewellery, handicrafts, auto engineering, banking and financial services, IT and ICT, and mines and minerals.

According to RMoL data, 1,46,000 youth (1,20,000 males and 26,000 females) were trained between January 2014 and October 2016. Thus, women account for only 18 per cent of those trained.

Constraints, Strategy and Issues[9]

The existing vocational training including skill development programmes offered by RMoL face several constraints. The number of seats available per thousand youth is the lowest. There is no flexibility in the duration of courses offered, dates of admission and examination. There is no diversification of the courses offered. The institution has failed to link the trained youths with industries. Examinations and certification of the youth receiving formal training are absent. A large number of posts of master trainers are vacant. There is no training institute for organising training of trainers. The instructors have no opportunity of scaling-up their own competence.

Only a small proportion, about 1.5 per cent, of the workforce in the age group of 16-20 has obtained vocational skills through formal programmes. A strategy to move forward to achieve policy targets needs to be in place, comprising the strengthening of administrative and management systems; establishment of trainers' training

9. *Source*: Power Point presentation "Skill Development Progress and Future Plan", RMoL (2015).

institute; revamping the existing; evolving modular courses of short duration; establishing a variety of academies and institutions in the public-private partnership mode; strengthening district computer training centres and the university-managed Krishi Vigyan Kendras.

RMoL currently faces problems related to manpower and budget for office; budget for strategic investment and expansion of skill development programmes; effective implementation of schemes launched by various ministries of the Central government which have funds but not delivery systems; overlapping of training programmes run by the Ministry of Labour and Employment and the Ministry of Human Resource Development; improper monitoring and assessment systems; and non-availability of master trainers and training institutions. These need to be addressed on a priority basis.

Conclusion: Can Linkages be Drawn?

The concluding part of this paper attempts to address the conundrum it began with: If the literacy levels among the youth are low and huge gender disparities exist across rural-urban youth on the one hand and the SC-ST youth on the other, what are the possibilities of their having access to employment in the job market becoming ever tougher? To what extent can the low educational levels resulting in low employment opportunities be enhanced by skilling and capacity-building? Can youth with low literacy and skills acquired in government or private institutions address its unemployability adequately?

Expectations from this demographic dividend of youth are very high in terms of social responsibility and citizenship. Is it fair to expect the youth to fulfil this role without drawing the linkages and addressing the gaps? Though the paper does not aim to answer these questions, the work of two NGOs/CBOs (non-government organisations/community based organisation) in the state working specifically with youth is highlighted, as an attempt to provide an insight into some of the issues raised.

Vishakha

Vishakha emerged out of women's movement in Rajasthan in 1992. It has been working on issues of empowerment, gender equality and self-transformation since its inception. In the process, it started working on empowering men and youth groups, both male and female. The emphasis is on understanding the self; analysis of the situation related to the individual as well as of surrounding systems, making informed choices/decisions, access and control over resources and collective-building. For combating violence, Vishakha adopted a strategy of moving from relief to empowerment as its ultimate goal is to attain well-being through empowerment.

Vishakha has been working with young girls (11-19 years) in the Salumber block of Udaipur district and with young adults/youth in Bagru and Jaipur. At Salumber, Vishakha works in 247 villages and 362 AWCs with out-of-school adolescent girls to empower them to challenge and question patriarchy and related discriminatory social norms. The exercise is carried out with collaboration of individuals, local community, administration and various service providers. Rights-based discussions and dialogues are organised at village-level through a curriculum developed with the participation of various key stakeholders. UNFPA and the department of women and children's development provide support.

The work with youth is implemented through youth resource and well-being centres in eight colleges of Jaipur city and Bagru block. Roughly 40-50 youth access these centres daily for counselling to deal with their inter- and intra-personal issues and internet and library use. They participate in various capacity-building activities including issue-based discussions, training, games and hobby classes. A large majority of issues relate to career-based counselling, intimate relationships, family issues, sexuality, self-harm and substance abuse. Workshops on different issues such as community-level reporting and journalism, dance, drama and theatre, photography, psychotherapy (object theatre) are organised. This work is supported by National Foundation of India.

Jatan Sansthan, Railmagra Block, Rajsamand District

Since its inception, most of Jatan Sansthan's work is aimed at improving the social and demographic status of the population of the selected area with a special focus on young people. The programmes for youth are implemented through formation of youth groups/clubs, and associations as well as through a strong network of youth volunteers. Jatan is also working to enhance youth participation in local governance and public services, as well as providing opportunities to young people in the community to design and implement programmes catering to their health and development needs, and skill-building of rural youth to provide better and improved employment opportunities. Jatan has created a platform for young people to voice to their concerns and find solutions for them. Jatan offers regular opportunities to young people to participate at both national and state-level conventions on sexual and reproductive issues and rights.

Under Project Hilor, the organisation is working with the out-of-school adolescent 10-19 year-old girls in Udaipur district. It addresses complex issues of marriage at an early age, school dropouts, skill empowerment and social consciousness. Its strategic approach comprises awareness building in areas of social, health/reproductive health and financial literacy. The implementation is coordinated through the directorate of women's empowerment as part of the large-scale SABLA initiative.

Linking youth to organisations/projects like these could provide solutions to some of the dilemmas faced by the youth in the existing situation. Doubtless, the work of organisations, such as the two-cited above, needs to be replicated and multiplied.

9

AMIT KUMAR

Perceptions of Rural Rajasthani Youth: Education, Livelihood, Citizenship

Case Study of Youth in Chandel Kalan, Chaksu, Jaipur

Introduction

The current young generation will play an important role in the future of their localities as well as larger communities. They have the potential to influence positively social, economic and political aspects of the society. Knowing their views, vulnerabilities, and perceived obstacles makes it possible to understand better the directions of improvements needed to enhance their future. Development is now connecting rural life to the urban more than ever before. Changes in the economies of local regions follow, as industries begin to shift according to emerging market demands. Increased education is raising expectations for those in the job market. These trends directly affect the lives of the new generation of the youth. Their success depends on their ability to negotiate societal transformations.

This paper discusses results of a survey of rural youth across 10 villages in Rajasthan. The survey provides insights into concerns of the rural youth and the self-perceived status. Views of the youth are juxtaposed with an analysis of actual conditions in the state in this paper. It concludes with recommendations for necessary action on the basis of the realities the youth have inherited and their reported responses to those realities.

Educational Status of Youth and their Perceptions of Schools

School attendance in Rajasthan villages is on the rise, literacy rates are increasing, and average education levels are rising. However, it seems that the rural youth do not see much benefit in pursuing education beyond basic or intermediate levels. Several reasons explain this. The youth report that access to secondary and senior secondary schools is difficult because of their distant locations. For example, there are primary schools in all 10 villages in one *panchayat* near Jaipur but there is only one senior secondary school. Just 12 per cent of the youth in all 10 villages passed the secondary school examination and less than 5 per cent reached the plus-two level. This is an issue for all youth in the survey.

For girls, there is an additional hurdle, as most families will not send their girls to schools outside the village. The number of girls and boys attending schools is similar between the 6th and the 9th class; however, none of the girls covered by the survey had passed class 12. Girls report that co-educational classrooms above class 8 are uncomfortable for them. They said that separate classrooms for boys and girls, as well as school locations closer to villages would increase their attendance at the secondary and higher levels. The lack of female teachers is also a concern.

Declines in school enrolment at the secondary levels for all youth also seemed to be due to a feeling that school attendance did not translate into practical benefits. Respondents claimed that increasing loads of work and home responsibilities did not allow them to afford the time, effort, or expense involved in attending school. A common theme was that the educational system did not provide access to future employment. Most of the rural schools reportedly focus on arts or commerce rather than science and mathematics streams that lead to career possibilities. Sixty per cent of the girls reported that their schooling involved no career training at all, while 31 per cent reported that they were trained in stitching and *nagina* work. Only two girls in the entire *panchayat* of 10 villages had received computer training that might translate into a career. Among the boys, 31 per cent received computer training while 26 per cent received no training. The remaining boys received training in agriculture, driving, and *nagina* work.

It is evident that the rural youth do not have access to quality education that would prepare them for future employment. The youth themselves see the disconnect between education and future employment outcomes. Consequently, they seem to have lost confidence in its value.

The youth who are high school or higher secondary pass report that they are no longer interested in manual labour jobs that typically engage adults in their villages. They yearn for jobs that earn more. They have been led to believe that their educational efforts should result in white-collar jobs such as clerical work. In addition, many in the job market yearn for government service, but clerical and government jobs are few and the competition is high.

Youth Economic Status and Perceptions of Livelihood

Villages with roads have become well connected to urban areas. Closer connections to cities have brought in their wake urban culture to rural communities. Often, the status of a village is related to its roads and or mobile towers. As transportation is an important requisite of development, villages without access to roads remain relatively backward. This development has brought some new businesses to the communities as well. Often situated along connecting roads, these new businesses come in the form of mobile recharge centres, photocopy shops, restaurants, and banks. However, modern industrial and manufacturing concerns have yet to relocate to rural areas.

The youth surveyed report that despite such developments, their job prospects have not significantly improved. Overall, their sentiment is that job opportunities in the formal, organised sector remain low. Almost 40 per cent of the employed rural youth worked in agriculture. This is a tenuous enterprise given the soil and water conditions in the state. Another 40 per cent of the employed rural youth worked as daily-wagers in unskilled occupations such as construction and piece-meal handicraft. Ironically, with urbanisation and development, manufactured goods are overtaking local village products even in the villages and packaged food products are replacing local fruits and vegetables in village kitchens. In other words, under the influence of urbanisation, local professions face a downturn, but modern industries are yet to make it to the rural communities. This does not bode well for rural youth. They feel they are not being educated to engage in meaningful employment and whatever informal rural employment that used to exist, has been endangered by the influx of urban products.

Another significant finding of the survey is that the youth are frustrated about finding within their village mentors who can help them search for jobs and livelihood amidst these economic changes. They do not believe that government employment schemes are meant realistically to increase the livelihood security of rural communities. Only 45 per cent of the youth reported being registered for work under the Mahatma Gandhi National Rural Employment Guarantee (MNREGA) Scheme with only a few currently employed through the programme.

These direct economic effects are accompanied by indirect societal changes as well. The youth reported that every village household now considers mobile phones and televisions as necessities. The desire for material goods significantly increased the spending of the people in these communities on expensive yet non-essential items. Almost every male youth in the *panchayat* reported a desire for the ubiquitous leading brand motorcycle. Social pressure to achieve prestige in the village leads to purchase of luxury items, and especially, high marriage expenses. The rural youth feel it acutely.

Liquor shops have become commonplace with easy import of alcohol from cities. Over 70 per cent of the young men reported routine use of liquor and tobacco products including *beedis*. According to one survey, there are now more liquor shops in villages than there are vegetable shops. Liquor consumption was a matter of great concern among women, especially in light of the linkage between drug and alcohol use and incidence of domestic violence.

Youth Political Status and Participation in Government

Despite the low job prospects in villages, many youth remain in their home villages. Only 31 per cent of the young male population surveyed had moved out of the district for employment. Movement of females is commonly more restricted, and only 16 per cent of them had migrated out for a livelihood. These statistics might suggest a closer youth affinity to their home villages; therefore, their vote and participation in local government could be of significant influence, if properly mobilised.

The youth in Chandel Kalan *gram panchayat* appear to understand their political rights, as 85 per cent of them had received the Election Commission electoral photo identity cards. Most of them actively participated in elections. Despite some hesitation about candidates and parts of the political process, the youth seemed to believe that the voting in their community was a fair process. Nearly 97 per cent of the boys and 87 per cent of girls believed that they voted without pressure or fear.

They did express some valid concerns about the political process. Some believed that since a party system in *gram panchayat* elections creates unnecessary societal discord, such elections should be party-free. In fact, nearly 60 per cent of the surveyed youth population felt that irrespective of the party governing the state, there would be no improvement in their village/neighbourhood. Less than 1 per cent of rural youth were associated with a political party.

Youth participation in local government apart from voting and campaigning is limited. They have some involvement in non-political organisations, but most of this is on an issue-by-issue basis. These are normally small acts. Most youth reported never having been involved in political activities such as election rallies or political protests. This is especially true for females. As the *gram sabha* is often controlled by a few powerful people who do not readily inform the public of proceedings or meetings and is rarely run in a proper fashion, the youth normally have little involvement. This is unfortunate, since *gram sabha* meetings could be a good platform for the youth to express their views and participate in local governance.

Conclusions

Understanding the struggles and outlooks of the current youth population is important, while addressing changes needed in the society, as they are the future leaders of society. Perceptions of the youth on education, livelihoods, and citizenship all provide critical information:

i. A quality education that prepares one for employment should be available to all students. A successful graduate should be confident of his or her ability to secure a job. The education system is hard to access geographically and is not necessarily preparing them for livelihoods. If this continues, it is possible that fewer students will attend school as it adds little value to them as workers. However, access to vocational training in schools offers a possible solution to this problem as it could lead to real world skills. It would also help establish new industries in rural areas to employ youth. Most youth are interested in pursuing meaningful vocational training. In addition, the gender gap in attendance requires special attention, since females are significantly less likely to go to school due to distance and concerns for safety and social norms within the classroom.

ii. Vocational training is essential for offering stable and sustainable livelihoods. Training should be based on market needs and potential for expansion of industry within a community. Accessing existing government schemes of training, development, education, health, and advocacy should be a priority for village leaders.

iii. The youth need to be encouraged to take part in political processes beyond voting. They have the potential to make important changes, both within the *gram sabha* meetings and through elected positions. Most youth look to those in government or politics and *panchayat* officials for support in searching for jobs. Young people could play meaningful roles in elections, actively voting and campaigning. The overall youth influence and contribution to party policies and vision is currently limited in a system that functions according to seniority, but youth numbers would be a formidable demographic when properly mobilised.

In conclusion, rural youth occupy a tenuous position economically, they struggle educationally, and they participate marginally in local politics. The results of the survey on rural youth in Rajasthan lead to a call to address the issues of education, livelihood, and political participation. Several groups such as the Rajiv Gandhi National Institute of Youth Development profess the goal of empowering youth to make active contributions to act as change agents in society. By addressing these issues, the society can share those goals and support the young generation in becoming change agents who can make positive and lasting improvements within their communities.

10

SWETA MISHRA

Odisha Youth Policy

Tracing the Journey from Formulation to Implementation

Formulation of Odisha State Youth Policy (OSYP)

Odisha is passing through a demographic transition with 42 per cent of its population in the age group 13-35 years. The youth represent not only a productive segment of the society but also its most innovative, enterprising and optimistic dimension. Both these are crucial in shaping the present and future performance of the state, in achieving inclusive growth and development. The youth needs focussed attention to take advantage of the demographic dividend and help channelise its energies to build a better future. The Government of Odisha launched the OSYP in April 2013, aiming at responding to the needs and aspirations of its young people and creating an enabling environment for them to better engage in the development processes. The overarching goal of OSYP is to engage, enable and empower the youth to be partners in the development process. Building human capital requires working across many sectors with an integrated approach and establishing lines of accountability for youth-oriented outcomes. Therefore, the government has subsequently intervened to intensify initiatives/programmes of various departments to encourage youth development.

The United Nations Population Fund (UNFPA) in Odisha has been a partner of the government to ensure a participatory process to guide the policy development. It was designed by adopting a systematic approach involving an extensive qualitative study and a series of consultation meetings at the state, regional and district levels with key constituents, stakeholders and special interest groups. Social media and the United Nations Solution Exchange Platform were used to make it broadbased, besides offline responses. Nearly 14,000 people contributed to the formulation process. The consultation involved young boys and girls, men and women, representing civil society organisations, government, and non-government bodies, Panchayati Raj Institutions (PRIs), the legal fraternity, corporates, media and self-help groups (SHGs). A diverse group of youth ranging from the academia to urban slums minorities, schedule castes (SCs) and scheduled tribes (STs), migrants, youth in conflict with law, sufferers from social and moral stigma (transgender, people living with HIV/AIDS), the disabled and numerous others were engaged in this process.

The policy formulation adopted a three pronged approach as detailed below.

Qualitative Study

A qualitative study was designed to understand the issues, concerns, aspirations and challenges of the young people in order to fulfil their potential. It covered 2,404 people (1,178 men and 1,226 women), 224 group discussions and 448 in-depth interviews in seven districts, 28 blocks and 112 villages.

Figure 10.1

Policy Formulation: Three Pronged Strategy

State, Regional and Districts Consultations	**Qualitative Studies**	**Virtual Platform Feedback/Communication**
State Level Consultations-10 Regional Consultations-with Specific Groups District Level Consultation-25 (Including Thematic Consultation)	Parents, Guardians, Peers, Teachers, PRI Members	Website, Mailbox, Facebook
Consultation with Line Departments	Inputs From Youth or Risks Such as Youth in Prison, Substance Abuse, LWE Affected Area Minorities Group, Tribal Youth etc.	Electronic and Print Media, Inland Letters, Indepth Interviews

Consultation Meetings with Officials and Key Constituents

The Chief Secretary conducted a series of consultation meetings with secretaries of all line departments to provide inputs to the relevant thematic areas. A special consultation meeting was organised with the Ministry of Youth Services, Government of India, to seek guidance on policy development.

Developing a credible youth policy also depends on capturing the perceptions, attitudes, aspirations, needs and concerns of the youth of all social segments. A series of thematic consultation meetings were conducted to reach every segment of youth at state, regional and district levels, covering all 30 districts.

Figure 10.2

Consultation Meetings

Key Constituencies

State Level	District/Regional Level	Special Groups
• Youth with Diverse Educational Background	• 25 District Consultations	• SHG Women
• Young Girls and Women	• Regional Consultations with Specific Groups	• Tribal and Minority Youth
• Youth in Urban Slums	• Migrant Youth—Ganjam and Nuapada Districts	• Unskilled Workers
• Youth and Media	• Tribal Youth—Koenjhar and Nabarangpor	• Unemployed Youth
• Youth and Corporate Sector	• SC Youth—Jeyapora	• Youth at Risk
• Judicial Officers and Lawyers		• Transgender
• Organisations/NGOs/CBOs Working with Youth		• HIV/AIDS Victims
• Youth Wing of Political Parties and Student Leaders		• Representatives of Political Parties

Review of On-line Media and Written Responses

The policy was given wide publicity through newspapers, radio and television channels and banners in public places to elicit young people's views on it. On-line responses were reviewed through the website, Facebook and the Solution Exchange platform of the United Nations. Handwritten responses and e-mails were also reviewed.

Characteristics of Participants and Respondents

The aim was to ensure fair and equitable contribution and representation among the participants with respect to the socio-demographic characteristics of the state. Efforts were made to ensure that women provided at least half the responses, but only 39 per cent of the responses were from them. The rural population accounted for nearly two thirds of the responses, commensurate with its share in state population.

Figure 10.3

Participation Analysis and Profile

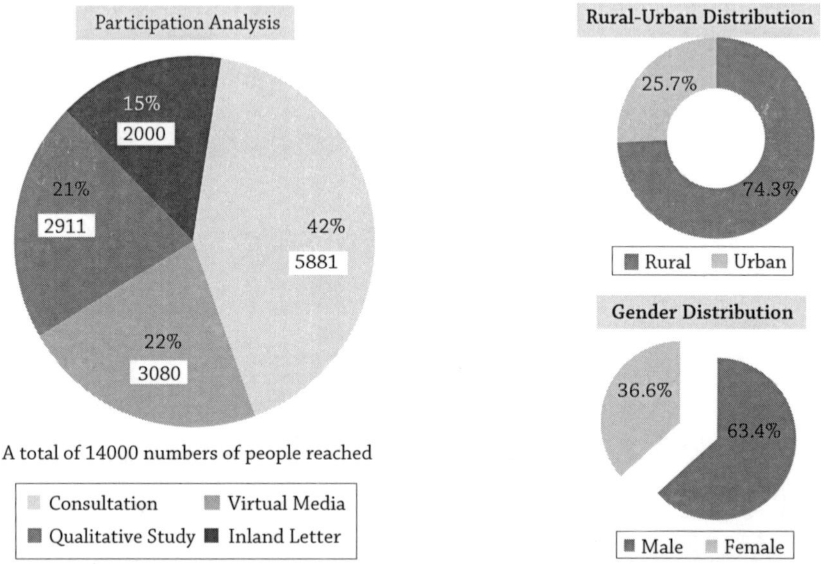

A group of experts developed a systematic plan and guidelines for the collection and analysis of responses. They were categorised under nine critical thematic areas of the policy. Education and life skills, followed by employment and entrepreneurship, received the highest attention of the participants.

Figure 10.4

Participants Responses on Thrust Areas

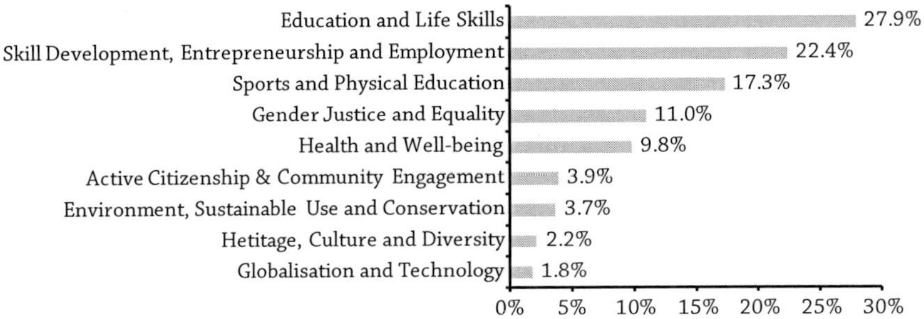

Contents of Odisha State Youth Policy

Definition

The policy defines youth within the age bracket of 13-35 into three sub groups:

Age Group	*Sub-Category Composition*
13-19	Adolescents whose needs and concerns are different from others because of their critical transition from childhood to adulthood.
20-25	Youth who are in the process of completing their education or are outside the system and engaged in paid or unpaid work.
26-35	Youth who are expected to have been settled but have not found livelihood opportunities and clear directions.

Rationale

Odisha has a distinctive culture characterised by a long tradition of tolerance, peaceful co-existence, respect for diversity and pursuit of excellence. OSYP seeks to build on the foundation of these values and create the social capital essential for achieving a sustainable and humane social and economic order. It aims to:

i. Capitalise on the demographic transition which presents the state with a historic window of opportunity to enable, engage and empower the youth for building a vibrant and prosperous Odisha;

ii. Guide different departments of government by aligning their initiatives, programmes and policies to encourage youth development and youth participation, as well as for bridging the gaps, and improving the effectiveness of existing interventions;

iii. Expand opportunities for youth through appropriate programmes and judicious investment in the youth, taking into account their needs across sub-groups and thrust areas;

iv. Provide the youth with tailor-made policy and programme responses, even as the diversity among them is recognised.

Institutional Mechanisms for Implementation

The policy contains 74 directives across 9 priority sectors and is implemented by 21 line departments. The department of sports and youth services is the nodal agency for tracking policy directives and activities of other departments with significant programmes/schemes for youth development. It is charged with responsibilities for inter-sectoral coordination, convergence of programmes and resources, and synergy in action.

A high power committee chaired by the Hon'ble Chief Minister has been formed to review the implementation on a half-yearly basis. A task force chaired by the Chief Secretary has been formed to review the progress on a quarterly basis. Further, a technical support unit has been established in the department of sports and youth services with the support of UNFPA, to facilitate tracking implementation.

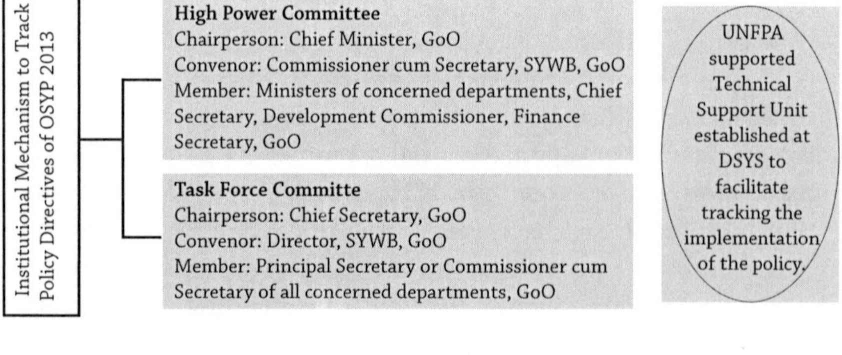

Partnerships with youth-related national and international agencies, civil society organisations, community-based organisations and the corporate sector are proposed to ensure convergence of efforts and resources. Regular and mandatory youth corps such as National Cadet Corps (NCC), National Service Scheme (NSS), Nehru Yuva Kendra (NYK), Indian Red Cross Society (IRCS), and Bharat Scouts and Guides will be actively engaged. Their on-going programmes will be augmented and new programmes and schemes will be introduced. Thus, the policy has been translated into a comprehensive plan of action with specific programmes and activities under each thematic area along with well-defined roles and responsibilities for the concerned departments.

Policy in Action

The first review meeting was held on 22 April 2013 under the chairmanship of the Hon'ble Chief Minister. Various departments were asked to share their action plans. A second review meeting was held on 3 July 2013 under the chairmanship of the Hon'ble Chief Minister to review the progress of implementation. The government had made a budget commitment of ₹400 crore to roll out the policy. In the last three years, many flagship programmes and schemes have been designed and the budget provisions have gone up. Task Force meetings to review the policy have also been held regularly under the chairmanship of the Chief Secretary.

The policy has 74 policy directives under 9 thrust areas, highlighted as below:

Thrust Areas	*No of Directives*
Education and Life Skills	9
Skill Development Training, Entrepreneurship, and Employment	13
Health and Well-being	9
Sports and Physical Education	12
Active Citizenship and Community Engagement	8
Environment, Sustainable Use and Conservation	4
Heritage, Culture and Diversity	5
Gender Justice and Equality	6
Globalisation and Technology	8

Flagship Programmes and Schemes

Subsequent to the announcement of the Youth Policy, key line departments launched many flagship programmes and schemes targeting youth empowerment and engagement. These are clubbed under the following broad heads:

Youth Leadership, Self-Empowerment and Development	*Skill-Building, Entrepreneurship and Economic Empowerment*	*Youth and Socio-Cultural, Environment, Heritage Development*
• Active citizenship programme • Youth internship programme	• Placement-linked skill development training programmes	• Encouraging involvement of youth bodies in environment protection programmes
• Integrated youth development programmes • Youth counselling centres • Sports and physical education, adventure sports • Youth festivals and exchange programmes	• Youth innovation fund • Scholarship to BPL/ST/SC/ deserving girl students for pursuing technical education in recognised/accredited institutions	• Training youth for disaster response and management • Training and engaging youth as eco-tourist guides • Dissuading youth from substance abuse
• Self-defence training for girls • Life-skill education	• Short-term certificate courses in accredited engineering and management colleges	• Training local youth at heritage sites for conservation and protection
• Campaign on substance abuse and m-cessation programme	• Scholarships and conveyance support to girls to pursue higher education	

Snapshots of Select Youth Empowerment Programmes

i. *Active citizenship programme*: This flagship programme of the department of sports and youth services aims to nurture a spirit of active citizenship and inculcate responsible behaviour among the youth. It was rolled out in 2014, covering about 3,000 educational institutions and 6 lakh youth in a phased manner.

ii. *Self-defence training for girls*: The plan, implemented by the department of higher education, is to train annually 2.5 lakh girls studying in colleges (+2 and beyond).

iii. *Internship programme*: Young boys and girls are exposed to the functioning of the government, to make them understand different development schemes and programmes, under the ambit of a youth empowerment programme titled Biju Yuva Sashaktikaran Yojna. This initiative provided 5,000 boys and girls from rural Odisha an opportunity to be attached to district and block administrative offices for three months with a nominal stipend.
iv. *Skill development and entrepreneurship programmes*: Placement-linked skill development training programmes (PLTP) are being taken up under the state employment mission. The programme targets school dropouts. It imparts training in varied skills. An on-line portal E-Nijukti registers candidates. Some 47,000 candidates have applied so far of whom 45,000 have been enrolled in various PLTP and 12,000 have been placed.
v. *Distribution of laptops*: Meritorious students from marginalised communities and poor families are provided laptops with prepaid data cards to encourage and enable them to meet their higher learning aspirations. The annual target is 15,000 students with more than 50,000 having benefitted so far.
vi. *Scholarships to ST, SC and deserving girl students*: On a pilot basis, 1,000 girls from below poverty line families pursuing vocational training in government industrial training institutes and industrial training centres are eligible to receive an annual scholarship up to ₹40,000 since 2013. Other girls are entitled to a soft loan of an equivalent amount.
vii. *Promotion of adventure activities*: This is a new scheme designed by the department of sports and youth services to promote adventure sports among the youth both in and outside Odisha.
viii. Involvement of youth bodies in environment protection programmes:

- *Disaster response and management*: A cadre of 10,000 college students has been trained in search-and-rescue missions and first aid. Additionally, around 6,000 youth have been trained to manage 135 multi-purpose cyclone shelters along coastlines of six districts.
- *Eco-tourist guides*: The tourism department has launched a new scheme to train identified young men and women as eco-tourist guides as a means of livelihood.

ix. Programmes for engaging youth collectives for road, fire and industrial safety, mapping and conservation of heritage sites.

x. *Building model villages free of alcoholism and substance abuse*: The health and family welfare department has launched a special awareness drive on substance abuse through the formation of 750 Red Ribbon Clubs.

xi. Young professionals programme for strengthening service delivery.

Key Learning and Way Forward

- *Inter-sectoral coordination and convergence in action*: Weak action coordination of an even coherent policy framework may result in limited outcomes. The successful roll-out of OSYP is due to a well coordinated governance structure. The involvement of ministers and secretaries of all the concerned line departments paved the way for an integrated approach. The institutional mechanism put in place enabled effective hierarchical and cross-sectoral coordination.
- *Institutional mechanism*: The institutional mechanism involving statutory bodies facilitated the emergence of an integrated approach ensuring convergence of schemes and effective implementation. Well-defined roles and responsibilities of key implementation actors at all levels have led to properly coordinated programmatic actions.
- *Monitoring and evaluation*: Ongoing reviews, objective periodic evaluations, and critical follow-up actions are crucial to successful implementation. A robust monitoring mechanism needs to be established using emerging

innovative techniques such as crowd-sourcing, participatory statistics, mobile data collection, micro narratives etc. Base-line surveys, longitudinal household surveys and ground-breaking studies in focused areas can also yield good results for tracking progress and identifying barriers.

- *Voice of youth in monitoring and evaluation*: It is equally important to engage the youth as development partners, encouraging them as leaders and ambassadors of advocacy. Listening to multiple voices of young people is a prerequisite of participatory democracy, good governance and service delivery.

11

ANJU DHADDA MISHRA

Building Blocks for Youth Policy

To reap India's demographic dividend, the youth has to be empowered with proper education, health and gainful employment. Young people also have to imbibe and cultivate a sense of social responsibility and accountability. This necessitates a wide range of interventions, which would be at the levels of legal, institutional, state policies and programmes. To be effective, all these interventions need to be accompanied by the necessary mindset change at the level of the individuals and the society.

The papers here have emphasised, and to an extent, spelt out the policy and accompanying programmes. It has been suggested that simultaneous efforts would need to be made to create an environment where the community, particularly the youth, would 'own' the proposed changes. We summarise below recommendations implicit in these papers. Our focus is on the state policy. We reiterate the importance of adopting stakeholder perspective in youth policymaking. The youth should realise that they are the locus of change that lies within them.

The state policy for youth should adopt an integrated approach to youth development, yet also identify key interventions which would lead to the desired change. Four areas identified for concerted action by the state as well as community are education, health, livelihood and citizenship, the last being broadly described as responsibility towards the society. We summarise key aspects that need particular attention in each of these areas in the paragraphs to follow. These are mostly culled from the papers and case studies in this volume and the consultation with the stakeholders mentioned in the introduction.

Education

If we wish to reap the benefits of youth-dominated demographic structure, the first and foremost need is to reform our education system. The present system has failed to produce high quality scholars, productive workforce or sensitive human beings. It has created a gulf between our homes and our schools and the schools and the real world. With misplaced emphasis on modernisation, it has led to a loss of self-confidence, especially among the new generation of students. Therefore the urgent and the most important need of the day is to put in place a system of education that inculcates a sense of responsible choices, an emphasis on justice and a capacity for creativity and innovation with a true futuristic outlook.

Some aspects of education that need to be looked into and addressed at this juncture are:

i. Absence of creativity education and structured lateral thinking training.
ii. Low emphasis on art and aesthetics, especially in rural areas.
iii. Poor quality or absence of science, mathematics and English teachers in government schools.
vi. Lack of opportunity for life and learning interface.
v. Lack of self-directed learning skill inculcation.
vi. Paucity of adventure, exhilaration and recreational opportunity in education.

Guiding principles: Education should aim at making students better human beings with high levels of sensitivity towards fellow citizens. It should also at the same time ensure livelihood skills and lifelong learning capacity. It must inculcate in the youth a respect for all cultures and pride in the diversity of this country. It should encourage a positive view towards our traditional values and customs, and at the same time, enable learners to question norms and practices that are discriminatory and divisive. These objectives, in addition to the capacity for creativity and responsible choice-making, should serve as criteria to evaluate curriculum and pedagogy.

Access: Common and quality education has to be ensured for all through decentralisation of educational infrastructure and processes as well as seeking close collaboration with communities. It should create appropriate platforms for youth participation at different levels. To solve the problem of universal enrolment, the Right to Education Act needs to be better implemented. Every effort should be made to prevent dropouts before completing secondary schooling.

Along with the efforts at the school level, there is a simultaneous need for change of mindset of parents who should not pull their children out of school early and should support their children's aspiration for higher education. Access to common and quality education will serve as a powerful equaliser, in addition to being a very significant development input.

Content: While designing school and college curricula, there is a need to recognise difference between knowledge and information. Emphasis must shift from rote learning to the understanding of the fundamentals. The curriculum of training courses should be thoroughly revised to make them more relevant to real life situations. There should be an emphasis on developing curriculum aimed at enhancing life skills and learning skills at all levels, and especially on building non-cognitive skills such as grit, teamwork and optimism. Care needs to be exercised to eliminate burden and noise, that is, overloading of non-relevant content.

Education should stress co-operation and team-building instead of cut-throat competition. Involvement in sports, particularly team sports, should be mandatory and facilities should be provided to organise sports activities at school as well as college levels. Meritorious sports persons should get encouragement and recognition due to them. Sports also need to be promoted as viable career options for youth.

All students should be trained in skills that can become viable career possibilities along with basic education, say, from class 6 onwards; so that those who do not wish to pursue academic training alone, are given training of high standard in possible options, as in some advanced countries. More importantly, the idea of dignity of labour should be inculcated among students at all levels. They should be encouraged to learn at least one craft. They should also take part in community service involving physical labour. Learning about the values enshrined in the Constitution of India and understanding the rights and the duties of citizens should form an important part of education.

Sustainability: A very important aspect of the present generation of youth will be sustainability of all pursuits. It may not have been of much consequence in the growing years of the present generation of elders, but it will be the single-most critical factor in the lives of the young people as they grow up, and thus should be made a part of all teaching/learning aspects and life and livelihood training for the young. Over-indulgent lifestyles of the affluent need to be contrasted with an understanding of the biosphere's sustainability and a sense of justice and equal opportunity.

Flexibility: Good counselling and guiding facilities at school and school leaving levels are needed to enable students to decide about their future studies or careers. Flexibility should be provided for lateral movement from one stream to the other. The straight-jacketing of science, arts and commerce streams should be removed and students be allowed to choose the disciplines they wish to follow, especially combining subjects across faculties.

Link between primary, secondary and tertiary studies: There is a total disconnect between primary and secondary studies. This is even more so between secondary and college studies. These levels should be regarded as steps in a ladder, each related to the other. Those who wish to pursue undergraduate studies should not find themselves in an unknown territory. This has become particularly important as a large number of the students in secondary and undergraduate institutions now come from tier-2 and tier-3 towns, most of them being first-generation learners.

Involvement of stakeholders: The government has the primary responsibility of catering to basic needs such as education to all citizens. It cannot abdicate its responsibility even when private sector enters the field. In such a situation, its regulatory functions assume great importance. Besides, it has to ensure that the public institutions in education establish higher standards and provide better facilities. Civil society institutions and local self-government bodies have to perform both supportive as well as vigilance roles. The alumni of the institutions have to keep themselves particularly involved and engage with the functioning of their alma mater. The policy must also address the parents as they have pivotal roles in paying due attention to the education of their wards and their positive counselling, as also in encouraging them to be independent decision-makers.

Extra-curricular activities, sports and adventure: The present situation concerning most sports and adventure activities is rather grim. Sports agencies suffer a paucity of investment and face technological obsolescence. These issues should be attended to, so as to keep appropriate sports and adventure within the reach of the young. Their need for the youth cannot be over-emphasised. They sustain enthusiasm and exhilaration, the inalienable rights of the young. They are also important in inculcating attitudes of fair play and justice, aspirations and teamwork. They further enhance health and well-being and enable learning to take success and failure in one's stride.

Creative expression: Another aspect of the well-being of the youth is the freedom of expression and creative engagement. It is so not only of psycho-social health, but also an important stepping stone to coming into selfhood or chiselling one's identity for the young. This is another area that needs immediate attention. All young people should have access to and opportunities for creative expression in verbal and non-verbal formats, in audio-visual, literary and performing arts, including theatre, cinema and new media. There should be teachers, mentors and facilities sufficient to cater to the growing youth population.

Facilities available for NCC, NSS, scouting, YDC etc. at present are very meagre, as less than 10 per cent of the college population is meaningfully involved in these institutions. Their numbers as well as of those that they can cater to have remained more or less stagnant, while college enrolments have risen exponentially. Adequate funds should be allocated for these institutions. Students should be encouraged to join one or the other such institutions. Two new cadres could be created in colleges to increase students' involvement with society, namely environment and climate change corps, and disaster and emergency mitigation corps.

Engaging in at least one creative form of expression which can be evaluated independently and providing opportunity for at least one adventure sport could go a long way in establishing an emotional equilibrium for the youth need today.

Relationships should be built between students (the youth) and neighbourhoods (the society), to understand their social environment better. The young should be encouraged to participate in constructive activities in their immediate localities, including their neighbourhood schools.

Education delivery system: A shift in education delivery system is needed to ensure greater recourse to technology-enabled learning. Rural and urban areas need to be equally equipped as far as technology is concerned.

Credibility of institutions: It should be ensured that all academic institutions, public or private discharge their responsibilities with transparency, integrity and authenticity. A higher education promotion and regulatory board comprising eminent and credible educationists needs to be constituted for this purpose at the state levels.

Health

Health is a fundamental right of our Constitution under the Article 21, the Right to Life and Liberty. Its operative interpretation is that every human being has the right to achieve the highest attainable level of healthcare. Despite this lofty declaration, the fact remains that young people who come from economically vulnerable and socially excluded sections, experience severe health adversities, essentially because of the insufficient availability of wholesome food, safe water, secure shelter, hygienic physical conditions, inadequate knowledge about how to remain healthy and above all, access to quality healthcare.

Role of Government: Like education, health also needs to be treated as the primary responsibility of the government. On the basis of budgetary allocations, health does not seem to be considered a priority government obligation, and a substantial part of the health budget is spent on employee salaries and establishment charges.

Therefore, budgetary provisions for health-related activities should be raised from the current paltry 1.1 per cent of GDP to 2.5 per cent as a start. The establishment expenditure should be reduced from the current level of 70 per cent to no more than 40 per cent.

The public health system needs to be strengthened. Healthcare providers need to be trained to become gender-sensitive and sympathetic to the needs of the deprived sections, and to impart ethical and quality health services.

Nutrition and development: These concerns need close monitoring, from infancy to puberty and adolescence, with regular health checkups, to ward off developmental deficiencies early.

Community efforts: Communities should take the lead in preventive healthcare. They have a major role in preventing non-infectious diseases by building awareness about harmful effects of smoking, excessive drinking, tobacco-chewing, eating of junk food and so on. Local healthy traditions need promotion. People must be educated to get rid of all superstitions and orthodox practices causing ill health. Civil society institutions have also a big role to play.

Adolescent health: Attention needs to be given to the health of the adolescents, covering health education, reproductive health, measures to reduce stress, and prevention of drug addiction. Special consideration should be given to youth at risk and youth from underprivileged sections of our society. The sexual and reproductive health profile of youth in different states highlights their vulnerability. The position is particularly alarming in those sections of population where marriages continue to take place before the legal minimum age for both young women and men. Even as sexual relations are initiated early and within the context of marriage for large proportions of young men and women, sexual risk-taking before marriage is not unknown among young people. Despite this early onset of sexual relations within or outside marriage among significant proportions of youth, available evidence suggests that, their knowledge of sexual and reproductive health matters tends to be limited. Sexual and reproductive healthcare seeking is limited. Maternal care-seeking among married adolescent girls is far more limited than that among adult women.

As a part of the healthcare activities, special efforts should be made to cater to the needs of the youth, to educate youth on reproductive health. Services of advisors should be available at school and college levels. Issues relating to physical, mental and reproductive health should be openly discussed with the youth along with action as appropriate, at government and community levels. This will help prevent common health hazards.

Anxiety and stress reduction: A large number of young people are reported to be suffering from anxiety syndromes, depression and psychological disorders. A host of factors are responsible for this. Pressure to crack top ranked competitive examinations is a big reason of the stress. Another is job-stress in work-life balance. Youth also want to catch up with modern amenities and glitter. Earning more money is not stress-free. Therefore, anxiety reduction is a big area of policy intervention, which is sadly missing today. Efforts have to be made by all concerned to focus on removing negative influences on the youth and on enhancing positivity and happiness in their life. Enhancement of emotional and spiritual quotient in their lives will be helpful in this direction. Similarly, games and sports must be promoted as tools of stress-busting and physical fitness.

Drug addiction: This is rapidly spreading mainly because of stress factors, but also due to some social and cultural practices and absence of meaningful engagement with life, thwarted dreams and expectations, reality disconnects and absence of coping capacity and support structures. In some states such as Punjab, it has become a major threat. Dimensions of the problem and its manifestation are not fully recognised in the absence of robust data. The measures taken are casual, based on anecdotal data. The first requirement, therefore, is of a survey focussing on the extent of the malady and its root causes. Coping strategies emanating from its findings should be implemented on priority basis.

Some reports suggest that at least one out of six addicts wants to be cured. There is evidence also that psychological tests can predict vulnerability to drugs at an early stage. Therefore, such tests need to form parts of the regular health programme. Support, including medical care, should be available for vulnerable individuals to rehabilitate them with socially useful and productive careers. State governments need to provide medical centres attached to schools, colleges and youth activity centres. Governments should work closely with social and religious institutions, if need be, to move towards eradication of the drug menace

Village or *mohalla* level anti-drug committees are needed to help the state machinery. They must be empowered to report drug availability and offer steps to rehabilitate people who want to come out of addiction. They should be allowed to monitor local level health and education facilities from the perspective of drug abuse. They can also help in discouraging social practices that directly or indirectly promote drug consumption and addiction. Thus, they will help create social awareness and isolate those involved in drug trade.

The youth who are cured in the de-addiction centres are not always welcomed back in society and face difficulties in finding employment. Special government programmes to rehabilitate them and provide opportunities for gainful employment are needed to ensure that they do not relapse.

Controlling supplies: It is equally important to strike at sources of supply of drugs. The number of drug inspectors should be increased. They should also be trained to inspect and discipline pharmaceutical companies that manufacture and sell drugs under camouflaged names.

Inter-state understanding is essential to control drug-trafficking. Similar understanding is needed with countries with known large drug cartels, such as Pakistan, Afghanistan, and Iran among others. They should be persuaded about the mutuality of interest.

Employment and Livelihood

About 300 million people in age group 18-50 will be looking for employable skills while the market will be able to cater to less than 10 per cent. The following suggestions may be considered as means of facing this problem.

Reorienting education: Education at all levels should encourage dignity of labour. A head-and-hands disconnect has come into being in our education so that the educated do not wish to do manual/

physical work and those who work have poor education. This mindset can only be broken through inculcating respect for work early on. Everyone should be taught, beginning with school and all the way through college, to respect and practice physical work. Secondary school curricula should include vocational training along with its practical aspects. This can also be done partly through internships. An entrepreneurial perspective should count towards further admissions. Vocational choices may be given due weight, without diluting academic evaluation.

Opportunities in non-formal sector: Nearly 92 per cent of workforce is engaged in the informal sector. There are relatively unlimited opportunities in self-employment and small industries and crafts. They need to be respected. They should receive proper training. Students should be graded on the basis of skills. These activities should be given all necessary encouragement through credit, technical and infrastructure support, commensurate with their contribution to the employment created.

Upgrading productivity in traditional arts and crafts and agriculture: A number of traditional trades are on the verge of dying. Governments should provide technical inputs and financial support to them, including stipends to apprentices to preserve both the arts and the artisans. A large part of rural youth could work wonders in the areas of traditional arts and crafts and agriculture, if trained well and provided initial support, including post harvest management. Apart from training in existing institutions in these areas, on-site trainings should be given high priority.

Encouragement to entrepreneurship: Developing entrepreneurship should be emphasised in professional engineering and management training. The humanities, social sciences and entrepreneurship courses taught in most technical/professional courses (barring a few institutes) are too thin, rudimentary and minimalistic. They do not provide sufficient grounding in the subjects, or create a significant connect with the society, or adequately develop entrepreneurial abilities. This non-technical content of professional courses needs to be attempted with much wider domain knowledge and understanding of ground realities.

There should be a closer link between technical institutions and the new start-ups in every area. Technical institutions should provide outreach support to the community space they inhabit. They should also provide incubation support of solutions to start-ups in their areas and domains. An outreach cell to track community needs and match them to domain expertise should be established in every college. Students and faculty of technical institutions should get to work on real projects.

Financial institutions and banks have to be more forthcoming and supportive of entrepreneurships and start-ups. Such support may be considered as part of the banks' priority lending.

Skill upgradation: The incidence of unemployment is higher among engineering and management graduates compared to the uneducated youth, caused largely by a skill mismatch. Entrants to the job market must be adequately and appropriately prepared. Employers should offer training to new entrants to overcome the gap between available and desired skills, for at least 30 days as compared to the average of 21 days in global companies.

Soft skills: Skilling should also focus on soft skills in the wider sense and not merely in writing job applications and resumes in English. Life skills aimed at a holistic growth of trainees, 'abilities beyond skills', should form a part of the vocational training. Psychological intervention aimed at shifting the orientation towards learning skills and capacity-building, as well as encouraging young trainees to become entrepreneurs, is very important in the present scenario.

Closer collaboration with industry: The skill trainings presently provided on a large scale and the requirements of the industry are rapidly getting out of joint. The existence of a large number of spurious and dysfunctional training institutions further compounds the problem. As a result, while we have a large unemployable workforce, we do not have workers for the jobs on offer. It is not only at the lower end of the spectrum of the educated youth that such mismatch exists; it prevails also among professionally trained persons who face the spectre of unemployment. The large number of unemployed engineers and management graduates support this story. A fool-proof mechanism that tracks and project skills is needed so that the trainees and graduates can be absorbed soon afterwards.

Need for counselling: Employment exchanges should have counselling facilities also. They should double up as employment counsellors. Employment cells in training institutions should conduct employability surveys and interviews. They should help create employer-employee interface at all levels and even on occasions, organise broad-based awareness workshops.

Youth and Society

Civil society should be actively engaged in four key activities to promote youth development:

i. Creating new powerful youth interventions;
ii. Promoting the youth-centric lens by sharing best practices, and also sharing and promoting youth leadership across different platforms;
iii. Ensuring accountability of public and private institutions in living up to their promise and towards ensuring their policies and programmes cater effectively to the young people and the larger society; and
iv. Creating and nurturing different types of youth collectives to help organise and professionalise youth work.

There will always be a generation gap between young men/women and their teachers and parents. It needs to be bridged by respecting the youth, and their rights, like right to privacy, and involving them in discussion. This should be possible by providing them a fifth space apart from their legitimate spaces of family, friends, career/career-related education and leisure or recreation. Youth committees and groups at village and block level should be formed and supported with resources to initiate their own actions and to create their own learning and leadership spaces with the help of youth facilitators or community mentors to guide and facilitate.

Three areas pose severe coping challenges to youth today: career, livelihood and relationships. Most of the desperate actions that young people are driven to are on account of hardships caused by one or a combination of these factors. Young women and men need to workout strategies. They need to provide and be provided peer and community support and counselling, when faced with challenging choices or circumstances. Support agencies such as The Child Line or similar civil society support groups for adolescents and youth also could go a long way towards re-establishing the youth's confidence in themselves, their own coping strategies and peer and community support.

Social exclusion is another significant factor contributing to youth anxiety. A renewed strategy to cope with it is needed, along with support to improve their a lot. The mainstream youth must be sensitised of the plight of the excluded and encouraged to become their partners in their struggle for liberation and social justice, to raise the level of consciousness of the entire youth population.

Specific Measures

A few clear choices to achieve these objectives emerge from all the discussion so far:

i. To develop youth programmes that support the deepening of the experience of the constitutional values including those of equality, secularism, justice, democracy, and freedom. This can be nurtured by designing state-wide volunteer action, experiential community immersion and active citizenship programmes;

ii. To focus on inculcating awareness of all forms of discrimination through exposure programmes, community visits, diversity camps and engaging young people to act against gender-based violence through creative, state-wide youth-focussed and youth-led campaigns;

iii. To use popular culture and relevant media to discover young people's talents and use them for advocacy of a better society and public action against injustice;

iv. To initiate social leadership programmes that offer capacity-building as well as financial and non-financial support to young social entrepreneurs and social change agents, in different spheres;

v. To enhance young peoples' participation in democratic processes by inviting them to take leadership, and actively seeking their mandate and their voice in all forms of policy-making and programme design; and
vi. To promote the formation of youth-led advocacy spaces in the form of collectives and campaigns.

It is also important to make the youth aware of their responsibilities. An illustrative list would include:

i. Take up ownership of learning and self-development.
ii. Maintain high level of energy and strive to perform to full potential.
iii. Follow policy of honesty, kindness, and commitment.
iv. Respect diversity and gender.
v. Say no to substance use, racism, discrimination, and intolerance.
vi. Offer voluntary services for development of weaker sections.
vii. Protect environment and promote cleanliness.
viii. Promote and defend democratic values.
ix. Participate in democratic processes.
x. Act as peace agents to curb violence.

Process of Implementation

A policy is as good as its implementation. Implementation is easier if visibility is imparted. As the Odisha experience shows, the Chief Minister of the State being the chairman of the implementation committee gave the youth policy the needed importance and made the task of co-ordinating with different government departments easy. Such high profile setups make possible the aligning of different initiatives, programmes and policies as well as the youths' participation in them.

A youth policy will have several goals, which will have to be translated in specific programmes and initiatives, implemented by different departments. Their convergence with requisite resource allotment must be ensured for synergy in action.

Concurrent monitoring and evaluation of programmes ensures timely correctives to policy as appropriate. Defining well the roles and responsibilities of key actors for implementing various aspects of the policy is critical.

In conclusion, it is necessary to share a few thoughts on the immediate course of action. The first and most important step is to draft a Youth Charter, or a Charter or Bill of Rights and Duties of the Young for the betterment of themselves and the community space they inhabit. The state can take the lead in formulating this. Links can then be established with agencies and regimens put in place to ensure and evaluate implementation.

Gandhiji had hailed the youth as the future of the nation. He had exhorted them to be like salt that strengthens and protects us. Those of us who remember the salt satyagraha will understand how important it is to unshackle our 'salt' from the bondages of ignorance, ill-health, desperation and bigotry.